PUB WALKS ALONG
The Ridgeway

TWENTY CIRCULAR WALKS

Charles Whynne-Hammond

D1101104

COUNTRYSIDE BOOKS
NEWBURY BERKSHIRE

COUNTRYSIDE BOOKS
3 Catherine Road
Newbury, Berkshire

ISBN 1 85306 452 1

Designed by Graham Whiteman
Cover illustration by Colin Doggett
Photographs by the author
Maps by Glenys Jones

Produced through MRM Associates Ltd., Reading
Printed by J. W. Arrowsmith Ltd., Bristol

Contents

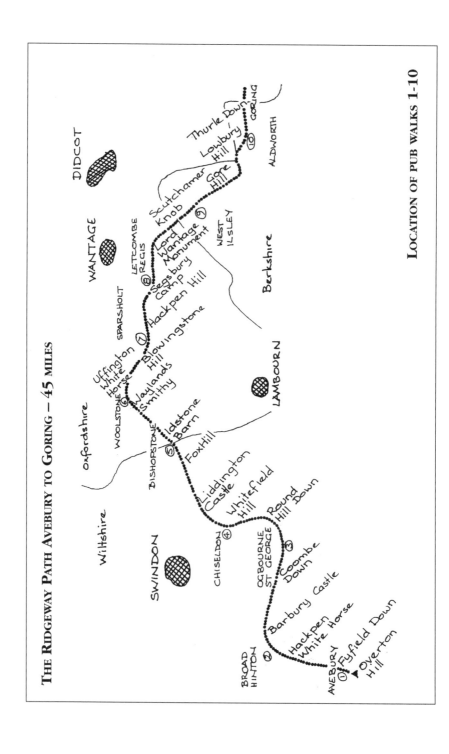

THE RIDGEWAY PATH AVEBURY TO GORING – 45 MILES

LOCATION OF PUB WALKS 1-10

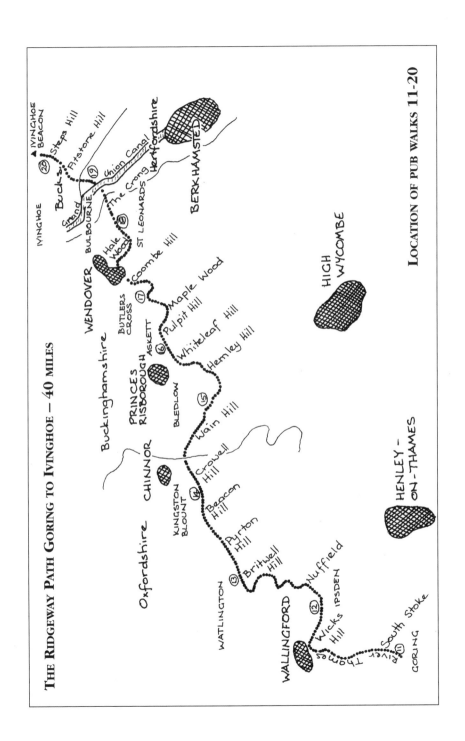

THE RIDGEWAY PATH GORING TO IVINGHOE – 40 MILES

LOCATION OF PUB WALKS 11-20

Walk

PUBLISHER'S NOTE

We hope that you obtain considerable enjoyment from this book; great care has been taken in its preparation. However, changes of landlord and actual closures are sadly not uncommon. Likewise, although at the time of publication all routes followed public rights of way or permitted paths, diversion orders can be made and permissions withdrawn.

We cannot of course be held responsible for such diversion orders and any inaccuracies in the text which result from these or any other changes to the routes nor any damage which might result from walkers trespassing on private property. We are anxious though that all details covering the walks and the pubs are kept up to date and would therefore welcome information from readers which would be relevant to future editions.

INTRODUCTION

The Ridgeway National Trail was designated in 1972 by the Countryside Commission. Today the Ridgeway is one of the most famous long distance footpaths in Britain, visited by thousands of walkers each year. From Overton Hill near Avebury in Wiltshire to Ivinghoe Beacon in Buckinghamshire this great way follows the chalk downland ridges of central southern England. For 85 miles (137 kilometres) it crosses some of the finest scenery to be found.

For present-day travellers, and especially walkers, the Ridgeway provides a unique opportunity to experience the scenic and archaeological wonders of rural England. From Avebury's ancient stones, to the hill-forts and strange chalk-cut horses on the downland slopes, the trail travels across the wide grassy summits to the Thames meadows. From there it meanders through the Chiltern beech woods encountering burial mounds, Iron Age earthworks and mysterious hillside crosses, eventually to climb the timbered ridges overlooking the Vale of Aylesbury. Here and there, on the way, nature reserves can be explored and wildlife studied, old towns and villages can be seen and National Trust properties visited.

The Ridgeway National Trail divides conveniently into two parts, roughly of equal length, at the river Thames. From Overton Hill to the Thames at Goring, the trail follows the route of the prehistoric Ridgeway. This ran along the escarpments of the Marlborough, Lambourn and Berkshire Downs and was a track used in the Iron Age, or possibly earlier, by traders. To the south this ancient ridgeway extended down through Dorset, to reach the coast at Lyme Bay. From Goring to Ivinghoe Beacon the National Trail follows the Chiltern Hills roughly along the line of, or parallel to, the Icknield Way, a prehistoric trackway linking the Thames with the North Sea. North-eastwards from Ivinghoe Beacon, the Icknield Way ran over Dunstable Downs and thence through Cambridgeshire to Norfolk along the East Anglian Heights. To the ancient Celts, the Ridgeway and Icknield Way together created the most important drove road in England.

The 20 circular walks in this book incorporate sections of the National Trail which, if added together, cover about half its total length. The remaining sections – the 'missing links' – are described briefly at the end of each walk, as a guide for those planning to combine circular routes and those undertaking the entire length. As an additional help to the latter, the maps in each chapter overlap so that they can provide a continuous link over the entire linear route. All the sections of the trail incorporated in the circular walks are described in the same direction, i.e. south-west to north-east. An acorn logo has been inserted in the relevant place in the walk directions to indicate where the circular walk meets the long-distance trail. The first ten circular walks cover the 'Ridgeway' half of the National Trail; the second ten cover the 'Icknield Way' half. In each walk the way to and from the National Trail is described, together with points of historic or landscape interest to be seen. Each walk is illustrated by a sketch map, designed to guide you to the starting point and give a simple but accurate idea of the route to be taken. However, for those who like the benefit of detailed maps, the relevant Ordnance Survey Sheet is very much recommended, especially for identifying the main features of the views. The relevant number of the O.S. Landranger series is given within each chapter of the book. All rights of way mentioned should be walkable. Readers who find any difficulty should contact the relevant authority, which is responsible for maintaining footpaths and bridleways.

Generally pubs still keep 'normal' opening times – 11 am or 11.30 am to 2.30 pm, and in the evening, 6.30 pm or 7 pm to 11 pm. Sunday afternoon opening, however, is now becoming common. Eating times tend to be 12 noon to 1.30 pm and 7 pm to 10 pm. Variations in these times are mentioned in the text. Most pubs have their own car parks and landlords are usually very happy to allow genuine customers to leave vehicles there while going for a short walk. All the pubs listed are friendly establishments offering a high quality of food and drink. Real ales are now widely available and menus invariably include choices for vegetarians. The food and drink items listed in the pub profiles are given only as examples. Regular dishes and daily specials may vary with the time of year and changes in kitchen staff. The beers and ciders too, may alter with contractual arrangements.

I should like to thank all those pub proprietors who supplied me with information. I am also indebted to Glenys Jones for drawing the maps and Jos Joslin (National Trails Officer) for giving me a plethora of background Ridgeway information. I should also mention Michael Woodbridge, who helped guide me round the Chilterns and Gwen Cassell who worked on the final draft.

Charles Whynne-Hammond

AVEBURY
The Red Lion

᨞᨞

*W*hat *a splendid walk this is! The great expanse of Wiltshire lies all around whilst above, hover the birds of downland - skylarks and meadow pipits, corn buntings and linnets. The outward route uses bridleways and footpaths that run alongside the river Kennet. These take the walker past Silbury Hill and close to West Kennett Long Barrow. The return route uses a byway, which is a wide, clear track. The Ridgeway section included in this circular walk is from Overton Hill (the National Trail's southern limit) to Fyfield Down, a distance of 2 miles.*

Avebury is a pretty village with an Elizabethan manor house, a church dating back to Saxon times and numerous thatched cottages. It would be worth visiting even if it were not famous as the centre for one of the most impressive prehistoric sites in Europe - a vast Neolithic stone circle that surrounds the village centre. Close by are stone rows, burial mounds and Bronze Age earthworks.

The Red Lion stands within the stone circle and is said to be haunted. It occupies a fine old building which boasts low ceiling beams, bare stone walls and tiled floors. There is one bar counter with many small rooms offering comfortable drinking areas. At the back a larger room acts as a restaurant and it is here where the food counter can be found. This is a Whitbread house so Flowers IPA and Fuggles real ales are sold. Other guest brews include Boddingtons and Wadworth whilst draught ciders are Scrumpy Jack and Strongbow. The wine selection is suitably varied. Bar snacks served include jacket potatoes and large baps, both with a wide range of fillings, and the main meals include steaks, meat pies, sausages, chilli-con-carne and traditional fish and chips. Pasta bakes and vegetable kievs would satisfy vegetarians whilst those with a sweet tooth might like to tuck in to toffee and apple fudge cake, spotted dick or treacle sponge. The Red Lion keeps normal pub opening times and welcomes children. Telephone: 01672 539266.

• **HOW TO GET THERE:** Avebury is 8 miles north-east of Devizes and 5 miles west of Marlborough. It stands on the A4361 road that runs south from Swindon, which is 12 miles away. The Red Lion is on the A4361 at the eastern end of the village.

• **PARKING:** There is a pub car park but vehicles can easily be left elsewhere in the village. There is a car park near the National Trust properties of Avebury Manor and the Alexander Keiller Museum in the Great Barn. There is a very large public car park south of the church, on the A4361 road towards Beckhampton.

• **LENGTH OF THE WALK:** 5½ miles. Map: OS Landranger 173 Swindon and Devizes (inn GR 102699).

THE WALK

The walk actually begins opposite the public car park on the A4361, reached by footpath from Avebury church. A bridleway signpost points southwards along the river Kennet and is labelled West Kennett Long Barrow. Follow the direction indicated along a clear trackway. In due course this trackway bends right to go through a gate. Go straight on at this point, over a stile. A narrow footpath now leads along several field edges. More stiles need to be climbed but the road is soon reached. Dominating the scenery along this entire length is Silbury Hill, which rises up on the right-hand side.

Of unknown date, but thought to be Neolithic in origin, Silbury Hill stands 130 feet above the meadows. It is Europe's largest prehistoric,

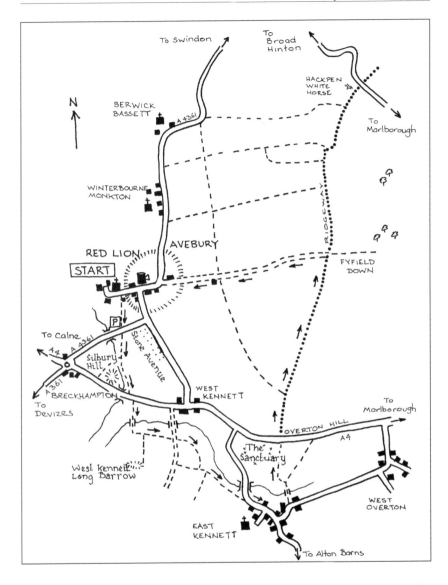

man-made structure. Although excavated many times, the site still holds its mysteries. Was it a burial chamber for a king or an important defensive site? Did it have a religious or an astronomical function? No-one yet knows.

The circular route continues on the far side of the road, almost opposite, and close to a thatched cottage. A signpost points the way up

Silbury Hill

a gravel track. This directs visitors to West Kennett Long Barrow. The track crosses a stream, turns left then right. Those not wishing to take a detour should continue straight on at the second bend, along a field-edge path. Those with time, however, should certainly digress to see one of the most impressive burial chambers in southern England. West Kennett Long Barrow dates from about 2700 BC, is 350 feet long and contains five separate caverns.

The field-edge path curves a little, passes through a gate and continues eastward as a clear, hedged track. Cross over the tarmac farm track and continue along the edge of the next large field, keeping the hedge to your right. In the far corner a stile leads through to a clear path through an area of undergrowth. At the next junction turn left along a wide gravel trackway. This crosses the meadows to emerge at a country lane. Turn right to walk through the pretty village of East Kennett. The start of the Ridgeway walk is now very close. Turn left along the lane signposted to West Overton and then, where this lane bends right, go straight on along a gravel track. Across the stream this track bends left then right to climb Overton Hill. The A4 main road is reached at the top, with the Ridgeway opposite.

Next to the A4, on Overton Hill, is the Neolithic site known as the Sanctuary. Concrete blocks now mark the holes, in concentric circles, where wooden posts and stones once stood. It is thought the rings had ritualistic functions, although no clear archaeological evidence has ever been unearthed to clarify this theory.

The Ridgeway path runs north from the Sanctuary as a clear, wide beaten-earth track. It climbs steadily across the open downland and the views improve considerably, especially to the west.

After 2 miles, but before the summit, a junction of paths is reached. To the right is a bridleway into the National Nature Reserve of Fyfield Down, which boasts one of England's largest tracts of high chalk pasture. To the left is a byway that runs downhill. Take the latter.

The way back to Avebury is very straightforward. For 1½ miles the clear trackway descends steadily. At first it is grassy, then it becomes rutted and chalky and finally, beyond Manor Farm, it is tarmac-covered. The Red Lion awaits at the bottom. On your way downhill you should see Cherhill Down on the distant skyline, if the weather is clear. This National Trust-owned hilltop is the site of Iron Age Oldbury Castle and the conspicuous Landsdown Monument.

RIDGEWAY - FYFIELD DOWN TO HACKPEN WHITE HORSE (2½ MILES)

The Ridgeway path continues northward from Fyfield Down as a wide, white earthy track. Beyond the summit above Fyfield it maintains height at around 850 feet, offering wonderful views across the Wiltshire Downs. Several trackways lead down from this section to the A4361, allowing walkers to plan their own routes.

BROAD HINTON
The Crown Inn

*A*n enjoyable walk with a variety of views, taking in the White Horse at Hackpen and an Iron Age fort, now a country park. The outward route uses a bridleway across fields, the return route uses a clear, beaten-earth trackway, and the ground is firm underfoot throughout. The Ridgeway section included here is from Hackpen White Horse to Barbury Castle, a distance of 2 miles.

Broad Hinton is a quiet and pretty place with a selection of thatched cottages and tile-hung brick Victorian villas. The church, though largely 17th-century, contains Saxon and Norman features together with a 15th-century tower. Inside are several interesting monuments including those connected to the Wroughton and Glanville families.

The Crown Inn is a large, plush Arkell's pub that prides itself on its food menus and well it might, for the choice is wide and inventive and the quality is excellent. Customers come from far afield to eat here.

To accompany your real ale (Arkell's 2B, 3B and Kingsdown), draught cider (Strongbow and Scrumpy Jack), or your wine or soft drink, you can have a bar snack or a full-blown multi-course meal. From sandwiches and ploughman's lunches upwards there should be something for everyone, including strict vegetarians. From starters like deep-fried brie, garlic mushrooms and pâté to fish and meat dishes, everything is home-made and mouthwatering. There is salmon, trout and mackerel; gammon steak and chicken; spinach cannelloni, lasagne and pasta bake.

The decor is traditional with a country feel. There are cushioned bench seats, some comfortable settees and nature pictures hung around the sides. Outside is a large beer garden with children's play equipment. Normal pub opening times are kept. Telephone: 01793 731302.

- **HOW TO GET THERE:** Broad Hinton is 6 miles south west of Swindon and 11 miles north east of Devizes. The A4361 Avebury to Wroughton road runs through the eastern edge of the village. The Crown Inn stands at the southern end, down the road from the church.
- **PARKING:** There is a large pub car park. Vehicles can also be left along the village lanes, which are not busy.
- **LENGTH OF THE WALK:** 6 miles. Map: OS Landranger 173 Swindon and Devizes (inn GR 104765). The distance can be shortened by omitting the White Horse from the itinerary and/or Barbury Castle. The Barbury Castle Country Park can be visited at leisure on another occasion.

THE WALK

Outside the Crown Inn turn right and then, opposite the way to the church, turn left along Post Office Lane. This leads all the way to the main road, which you reach facing the Bell Inn. Those who have not eaten at the Crown may like to sample this hostelry, for it is a friendly welcoming place offering a good range of real ales and bar snacks. Indeed, the village is not short of refreshment opportunities for close by at the petrol station is a pleasant little café. The bridleway leading to the top of the Downs will be found signposted alongside the Bell, close to a gravel lay-by. Take care when crossing the busy A4361.

The wide grassy track, rutted by tractor wheels and worn by horses' hooves, runs almost in a straight line across the farmland. The green slopes of the Marlborough Downs are directly ahead. All the while, large fields are over to the left. Immediately to the right are first a line of gardens, then a hedgerow and later a belt of trees. Beyond these you join a farm track for a short while. Where this farm track swings left continue

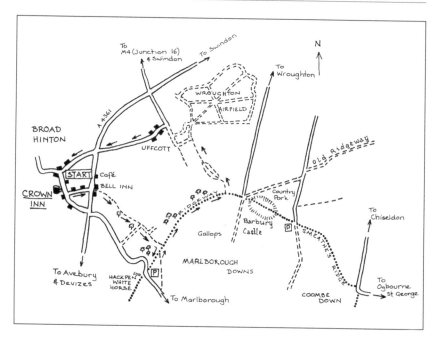

straight ahead, to make the final ascent. Through a farm gate on your way, climb the grassy hillslope alongside a wire fence, ignoring the tractor route that contours off to the left. Through another farm gate at the top you soon reach the Ridgeway path. Turn right for Hackpen White Horse, left if you wish to shorten the circular walk.

The top of Hackpen Hill is a pleasant spot and not surprisingly many motorists bring their cars here. From the gravel parking area wide views can be enjoyed across the river Avon towards the Cotswolds. Best seen from the Vale below, the White Horse itself was cut in 1838 to commemorate Queen Victoria's coronation. It was the brainchild of the Broad Hinton parish clerk.

The Ridgeway walk north-eastwards from Hackpen is splendid, with a wide panorama both sides. To the right is the rolling downland towards Marlborough, to the left is the upper Thames valley. Alongside the National Trail are three clumps of beech trees planted at intervals. There are many such clumps all along the Ridgeway, greatly enhancing the open chalk landscape. They were planted, originally, in the 18th century when the Ridgeway path itself was fenced and defined as a drove road. Such woodlands offered shelter for drovers and animals alike.

Beyond the third beech clump the Ridgeway descends to a col or dip in the grassy ridge. Here, below the ramparts of Barbury Castle, a country lane crosses the trail and there are some car parking spaces. The return to Broad Hinton begins in this col but Barbury Castle should really be explored beforehand. The entire hilltop is now a country park. At the far (eastern) side is a large car park, a public convenience, picnic area and an information board. Drivers can reach this hill from the Wroughton to Chiseldon road.

The Iron Age ramparts cover eleven acres and still form an impressive double earthwork. Historians tell us that the Battle of Beranburgh was fought on the slopes below in AD 556. In that bloody conflict the invading Saxons defeated the Romano-Britons, or Celts, thus laying the foundations for the new kingdom of Wessex.

The way back downhill begins along the Ridgeway, 200 yards west of the country lane. A signpost points north along a byway. The track is very clear, running as a rutted, grassy way between two large fields. Where the gradient steepens many different routes split off but these come together again at the bottom. Thereafter the track is wide and earthy. In due course it bends left and then, shortly after, right. In this way it keeps away from the many buildings occupying the old Wroughton airfield, an area which is private and fenced-off. At the road, turn left to walk through the hamlet of Uffcott and onwards eventually to meet the A4361. Cross straight over for Broad Hinton village centre.

 ### RIDGEWAY - BARBURY CASTLE TO COOMBE DOWN (3 MILES)

From the Barbury Castle Country Park car park the Ridgeway path runs south-eastwards along Smeathe's Ridge, affording wonderful views across the Og valley. Interestingly the National Trail leaves the original Celtic ridgeway, which takes a more direct route to Liddington Castle, via Chiseldon. The present Long Distance Footpath route crosses the Og valley in a large curve, following other ancient trackways that were used in prehistoric times when the flat meadows were impassable.

OGBOURNE ST GEORGE
The Parklands Hotel

A pleasant walk with very pretty views incorporating woodlands, quaint thatched cottages and chalk downland scenery. This route circumnavigates the village of Ogbourne St George, crossing the Og valley and keeping, generally, to the lower slopes of the Marlborough Downs. The way is very clear and firm throughout. The Ridgeway section included is from Coombe Down to Round Hill Down, a distance of 2½ miles.

The Ogbourne villages, along the pretty Og valley, boast a wonderful collection of old, thatched cottages and should be explored at leisure. Ogbourne Maizey has a fine Jacobean manor house, Ogbourne St Andrew has a Norman church and, in its graveyard, a Bronze Age round barrow. Ogbourne St George is the largest of the three and is now happily bypassed by the main road.

Parklands was converted to a ten bedroom hotel in 1989 but retains many of its old village pub characteristics. It is homely and friendly, serves a good range of real ales and bar food, welcomes walkers and is frequently full. It now has the added bonus of being open all day, so teas and coffees are permanently available.

Inside, the decor is smart yet comfortable. There is a small bar room at the front, a cosy lounge at the back and an attractive bare brick-walled restaurant to one side. Wadworth 6X and Arkell's Kingsdown Best Bitter are served (this being a freehouse) and there is a full wine list. But it is the food served that especially brings in the customers. From English traditional dishes, like cottage pie and Wiltshire pasties, to continental and Eastern cuisine, like chicken or vegetable Kiev, spiced lamb and tiger prawns, the choice is mouthwatering. Vegetarians too have a good selection from such items as spinach and tomato lasagne or fried vegetables with cream sauce. The chef is also happy to satisfy any particular dietary requests. Telephone: 01672 841555.

- **HOW TO GET THERE:** Ogbourne St George is 4 miles north of Marlborough and 8 miles south of Swindon. It stands next to the A346 which now has a raised bypass around the village centre. The Parklands Hotel stands around the corner from the Old Crown Inn, on the road that leads westwards.
- **PARKING:** Parklands has its own car park but vehicles can easily be left along the kerbside in front. The village lanes are wide and very quiet.
- **LENGTH OF THE WALK:** 4 miles. Maps: OS Landranger 173 Swindon and Devizes, 174 Newbury and Wantage (inn GR 202743). This walk crosses the edge between two OS maps.

THE WALK

Turn right outside Parklands and walk westwards along the main village street. There is a pleasant mixture of cottages here, some old, some new and many thatched. At the far end the road dips to cross the little Og stream and then curves around a double bend to leave the buildings behind. Those with time should make a detour to the church, turning right immediately after crossing the river Og. Dating back to Norman times the church was sympathetically restored in the 19th century, its medieval character being maintained.

The Ridgeway path is soon reached beyond the western edge of the village. Where the road bends sharp right, turn left where the Ridgeway signpost points the way. The green slope ahead rises to Coombe Down.

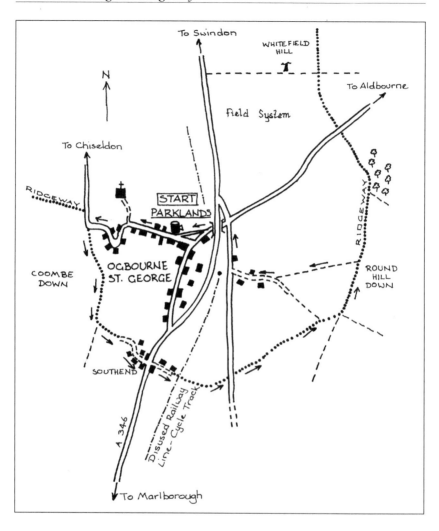

A very pleasant walk can now be enjoyed as the Ridgeway, here a rutted track of earth and grass, contours along between hedgerows. Down to the left, Ogbourne St George nestles in the valley. Beyond its scatter of cottages are the green slopes of Whitefield Hill, terraced with the earthworks of prehistoric field systems. In due course you turn left as the Ridgeway takes you down to the valley floor and the hamlet of Southend.

Crossing over the busy A346 road the Ridgeway continues on the far side of the valley. Still a wide grassy trackway, it climbs steadily, bending left as it crosses the line of a disused railway, now a cycle track and popular with horseriders and walkers travelling from Chiseldon to Marlborough. The ascent is long but not too arduous and the effort is repaid. To the left the view opens out northwards to the hills beyond Swindon. Across a country lane you continue to the summit where a number of bridleways lead off either side. Keeping to the Ridgeway path bear right at the first junction and left at the second. The views are, by now, all around: south across Savernake Forest and the Vale of Pewsey, east across the Downs and west back to Barbury Castle.

The Ridgeway now heads northwards towards Whitefield Hill, identifiable by its tall radio mast. You follow the National Trail for another ½ mile to a point, before reaching the distant woodland, where a byway signpost points left.

The return to Ogbourne St George follows a narrow grassy track that descends between two lines of bushes. The village is ahead and below. Towards the bottom of the slope turn right along a wider gravel track. This leads down past a commercial yard to the road at the bottom. To reach the village centre, across the A346, turn right alongside the main road and then left under the bridge. Parklands and the Old Crown Inn await.

 RIDGEWAY - ROUND HILL DOWN TO WHITEFIELD HILL (1½ MILES)

The Ridgeway Path continues northwards as a clear, fenced trackway. It climbs steadily almost the whole way, crossing a country lane on its way to Whitefield Hill, 850 ft high. Walkers can return to Parklands from there via a track down to the A346 and thence along the cycle track on the far side.

CHISELDON
The Patriots Arms
❧

Fine views can be enjoyed throughout this circuit, so bring your binoculars. The outward route includes a length of disused railway now converted to a cycle track which has become a haven for wildlife. The return route uses footpaths across farmland below Liddington Castle an Iron Age hill fort about 900 ft above sea level. The Ridgeway section included is from Whitefield Hill to Liddington Castle, a distance of 2 miles.

Chiseldon is a large village, but a peaceful one with a pretty church half-hidden in a combe and a scatter of thatched cottages around a maze of winding lanes. Two miles north, but within the parish boundary, is Coate Farm, on the edge of Swindon. This was the birthplace, in 1848, of Richard Jefferies the well-known countryside writer. The farm is now a museum.

Large and plushly decorated, the Patriots Arms offers exceptional comfort and service. The pub has separate areas for families, restaurant customers and public bar users. Outside is a large beer garden with children's play equipment. Everyone is made welcome, even small children for whom there is a special food menu.

This is a Courage establishment and so the real ales served include Directors and John Smith's bitter. The cider on offer is Blackthorn and there is a full range of wines – including a very good house red. But it is the food here that attracts the customers. From simple bar snacks to full, sit-down meals the choice is wide and delicious. There are burgers and jacket potatoes, baguettes and salads, home-made meat pies and curries, omelettes and pasta bakes, vegetable-only dishes and various fish platters. Desserts vary, but ice cream and cakes are normally offered and the coffee is very good. Normal pub opening times are kept but the landlord is happy to extend afternoon sessions when demand allows. Telephone: 01793 740331.

- **HOW TO GET THERE:** Chiseldon is 4 miles south east of Swindon town centre and 6 miles north of Marlborough. Junction 15 on the M4 motorway is only one mile away and the busy A346 runs along the eastern edge of the village. The Patriots Arms stands at the south-west corner of Chiseldon.
- **PARKING:** There is a large pub car park but vehicles can also be left, where space permits, along the road outside. The lanes here are quiet.
- **LENGTH OF THE WALK:** 7 miles. Maps: OS Landranger 173 Swindon and Devizes, 174 Newbury and Wantage (inn GR: 185795). This walk crosses the edge between two OS Maps. It should be noted that the total length of the walk can be shortened by using country lanes instead of paths and by taking a more direct route to and from the Ridgeway.

THE WALK

Turn right outside the Patriots Arms and walk east along the B4005. About 300 yards before reaching the main A346 road turn right down a signposted footpath. This runs down the edge of a large field. In the far corner a stile leads on to a country lane. Turn left. The disused railway line, which is now a cycle track, will be reached immediately before the A346. Follow this track south.

Wiltshire County Council, supported by the Countryside Commission, has designated a number of cycle trails throughout the Marlborough Downs. For the most part these use ancient tracks and bridleways but here the dismantled Swindon to Marlborough railway line has been adapted. And what a splendid route it has proved to be!

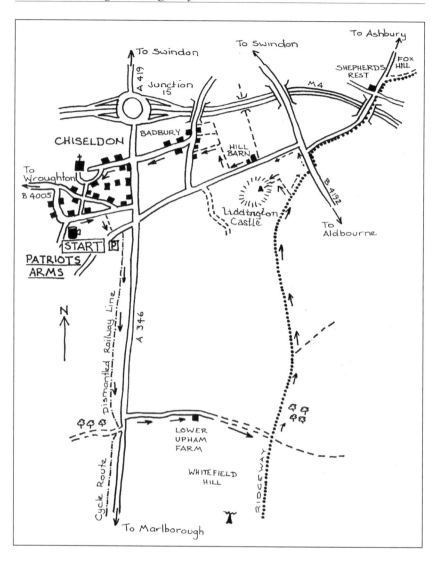

Either side of the firm, rolled-gravel path, mature trees and bushes provide a shelter belt full of wildlife. On the left the view is towards the steep green slopes of the Downs, on the right are the meadows stretching away to distant Barbury Castle. Follow this track for about a mile, until a belt of Scots pine trees is reached. Here walk up to the main road. Turn left and then, shortly afterwards, right, to follow a country lane signposted to Lower Upham Farm. Tarmac-surfaced at first, but later (beyond the farm) gravel-rutted, this lane takes you all the way to the top of the Downs, by way of a steady ascent. The Ridgeway path will be reached at the top. Joining from the right, as it descends from Whitefield Hill, the National Trail leads off to the left. Follow this direction.

 The wide, grassy track, rutted from vehicular use, heads northwards alongside some beechwood copses. The panorama to the west takes in much of northern Wiltshire, beyond the river Avon and Chippenham. After a short while the Ridgeway forks. To the right is a route signposted for vehicles, to the left is the route used by walkers. Following the latter you proceed to a gate and, thereafter, along the edges of a number of large fields. Liddington Castle is directly ahead. At the summit the Ridgeway curves right, around the head of a pretty, deep combe, thus missing the ramparts. Fear not, for a 'permissive path' is signposted off to the left. By a circuitous route around a field you can thus reach the earthworks.

The return to Chiseldon begins on the lane beneath the northern slopes of Liddington Castle. The steep grassy hill is privately owned but the local farmer kindly allows access to the earthworks. By public right of way the official route involves a return to the Ridgeway path and a descent to the B4192 where you would turn left then left again along a country lane. The footpath then to be followed leaves the lane west of the farmstead at Hill Barn. It runs between two large fields, towards the M4 motorway which is seen in the distance. After less than ½ mile another footpath, on the left, takes you to the thatched cottages of Badbury. From there, follow the country lane west to the A346. Crossing straight over this main road, to follow Butts Road, you can eventually reach Chiseldon church and the village centre.

RIDGEWAY - LIDDINGTON CASTLE TO FOX HILL (2 MILES)

This section almost entirely follows public roads. Descending from Liddington's summit the National Trail turns left along the B4192 and then right along the road to Bishopstone and Ashbury. Across the M4 motorway is the junction where stands the Shepherds Rest Inn. At this point the Ridgeway crosses the line of the Roman road which linked Cirencester with Silchester. The National Trail becomes a trackway again at the bottom of Fox Hill.

BISHOPSTONE
The Royal Oak

The views throughout this circuit are wonderful. The outward route includes Bronze Age earthworks and a quiet road walk to Hinton Parva followed by a very attractive ascent along a grassy bridleway. The return route follows a path along a deep downland combe. The Ridgeway section included is from Fox Hill to Idstone Barn, a distance of 2½ miles.

Bishopstone is the archetypal downland village. Nestling around a large central pond, beneath the chalky slopes, a collection of thatched cottages line a rambling network of lanes and alleyways. There is an old mill stream and the medieval church is half-hidden in a wooded combe. In former times a curfew bell was rung each evening to guide travellers lost on the Downs.

The Royal Oak suits the village admirably for it is the traditional English pub *par excellence*. Plain and simple, homely and friendly: the place is old-fashioned in the very best sense. Chess and cribbage leagues meet here, there is a regular Saturday evening sing-along around the piano and both children and pets are welcome. There is even a small village shop at the back of the premises. Inside there are wooden floors, old pictures and prints hung on the walls and a happy, heavy smell of food and drink. In winter months a woodburning stove keeps the place warm. Normal pub opening times are kept.

This is an Arkell's house selling 2B, 3B and Kingsdown real ales. Strongbow cider and a selection of wines are also on offer, as well as various stouts. The food served is especially good – from snacks to full meals the choice is wide. Soups, sandwiches and baguettes; burgers, chillis, lasagnes and curries; meat pies, fish dishes and pasta bakes can all make an appearance. Daily specials are very popular, like bubble and squeak, faggots and local sausages, and the puddings are similarly English and accompanied by custard. Organic meat from a local supplier is used and everything is home-made. Telephone: 01793 790481.

• **HOW TO GET THERE:** Bishopstone is 6 miles east of Swindon and 10 miles west of Wantage. It stands between the A420 Oxford road and the M4 motorway (Junction 15 being 4 miles away near Chiseldon). It can be reached from the B4000 at Ashbury. The Royal Oak will be found along Cues Lane, uphill from the village pond.

• **PARKING:** There is a pub car park at the rear, reached by circuitous route. Vehicles can also be left, here and there, along the village lanes provided no obstruction is caused.

• **LENGTH OF THE WALK:** 6 miles. Map: OS Landranger 174 Newbury and Wantage (inn GR: 245837). It should be noted that many alternative walks are possible from Bishopstone and the walk described here can be lengthened or shortened. Numerous paths lead up to the Ridgeway, all offering splendid walking opportunities.

THE WALK

Start by following the quiet road that heads west from Bishopstone and goes to Swindon. It curves uphill from the village pond, passing Church Walk on its way. Those planning their own walking routes should note that one bridleway leading to the Ridgeway will be found almost opposite West End Lane, another one is reached soon after the end-of-speed limit signs at the edge of the village. On the slopes below the top of the Downs you will see the grassy terraces or 'strip lynchets' that Bronze Age settlers cut to enable crops to be grown. When the sun is low these earthworks are impressive indeed.

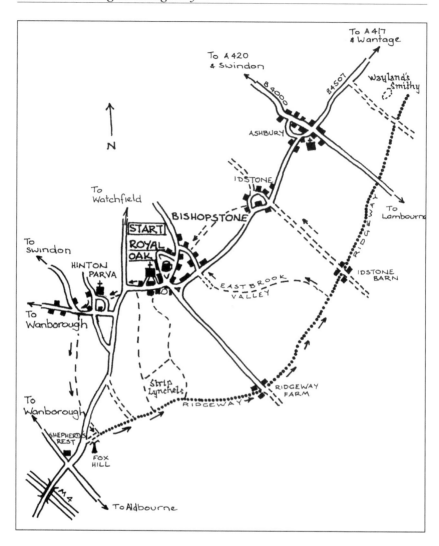

Keeping left at the road junction Hinton Parva is soon reached. A footpath signpost points the way right, up some rough steps and over a stile in the hedgerow. The route indicated crosses a couple of small fields diagonally, through kissing gates, to emerge at that part of the village near the church. From there a left turn brings you back to the Swindon road, where you turn right to reach the western end of the village. The bridleway required is signposted next to the village hall, close to a red telephone box.

The ascent to the Ridgeway is beautiful and should not be rushed. Beyond the village hall car park a wide grassy track leads up beside a hedgerow. Down to the right is a deep little combe where the short grass and uneven terrain offers a haven to rabbits. This area is owned by the National Trust and long may it remain unspoilt. Towards the top of the climb the bridleway veers left and the little combe veers away to the right. Keeping to the former you cross an area laid out for horse gallops, arrow marker posts showing the way along by the hawthorn bushes. Ahead is Fox Hill with its radio mast; behind is the widening view over Swindon. Across the country lane you continue along the bridleway to the top, where stands a large corrugated iron barn. Turn left along the Ridgeway.

At first the views north are blocked by Charlbury Hill but soon the whole panorama opens out. On clear days the Cotswolds can be seen across the upper Thames valley. The Ridgeway here is wide, firm and fenced, so the walking is easy. Up and down you continue across the folds of the chalk escarpment. To the half right you may get a glimpse of Alfred's Castle, an Iron Age hill fort, and Ashdown House, the handsome 17th-century mansion owned by the National Trust. Both are about 2 miles away.

Crossing a country lane at Ridgeway Farm you follow the Ridgeway all the way to Idstone Barn. Here a group of farm buildings cluster around a point where a bridleway crosses. Nearby a water tap and trough are provided for thirsty travellers. Stop awhile here to enjoy this lonely hilltop with open countryside all around.

The return to Bishopstone can be made by turning left at Idstone Barn, descending to the hamlet of Idstone and then walking across the meadows by footpath. There is a prettier and shorter route however. Retrace your steps along the Ridgeway by some 500 yards and follow the direction indicated. The signpost points north to Eastbrook Valley and Bishopstone. Next to the stile at this point, notice the wooden board announcing 'Oxfordshire'. The county boundary runs through here. Along the edge of the first field you continue into the second and bear left. The way is clear for you keep to the bottom of a grassy gulley which curves its way downhill. With 'access land' status this is truly a lovely spot. The steep slopes either side and the view ahead give a mountainous feel – a sensation not common in southern England. At the bottom, where the combe opens out, a gate leads through to a stony track that takes you down to the road at Bishopstone. Turn left for the village centre.

The village pond at Bishopstone

 RIDGEWAY - IDSTONE BARN TO WAYLAND'S SMITHY (2 MILES)

The Ridgeway path continues north-eastwards over Ashbury Hill, at which point it crosses the B4000 road that links Ashbury village with Lambourn. From the car park are views across the beech trees of Kingstone Combes, where the chalk escarpment has been eroded by several streams. Shortly before Wayland's Smithy the Ridgeway runs alongside a pretty belt of trees, offering shelter in windy weather.

WOOLSTONE
The White Horse

*T*his is classic Ridgeway walking, full of interest, encompassing an
ancient earth carving, a Celtic hill fort and one of the most impressive
long barrows in the country. The outward route uses footpaths across flat
farmland and a country lane ascent of the Lambourn Downs. The return
route uses a chalky track which descends steeply across sheep pastures
owned by the National Trust. The way is clear throughout and there are
superb views to be enjoyed. The Ridgeway section included in this
circular walk is from Wayland's Smithy to the Uffington White Horse, a
distance of 1½ miles.

Woolstone is one of the many pretty villages standing at the foot of the
Lambourn Downs. It has a little church, a cluster of thatched cottages
and a couple of busy farmyards. All is very rustic and traditional. So too
is the White Horse inn, which is round the corner at the bottom end of
the village.

This is a 16th-century building and is reputed to be one of the oldest inns in England. It is said that Thomas Hughes wrote *Tom Brown's School Days* here in the 1850s, and today the place continues to offer first-class accommodation. Inside, the atmosphere is dark and cosy with low ceiling beams, bare stone walls and old prints of local scenes. There is one main bar room but this is so arranged that separate lounge and dining areas are provided. At the rear is a pleasant enclosed garden.

The White Horse is a freehouse, serving various real ales such as Wadworth 6X, Arkell's 3B, Fuller's and Bateman's. The draught cider is Scrumpy Jack and a full range of wines is offered. From bar snacks to full meals, both à la carte and table d'hôte, the choice and quality of food served are superb. There are salads, ploughman's lunches and pâtés, steaks, pastas and pies. Amongst the fish courses are salmon, haddock and Japanese prawns, and amongst the vegetarian meals are mushroom quiche, tagliatelle and spicy Thai vegetable schnitzel. A full sweet menu, constantly changing, is also provided. The White Horse keeps normal pub opening times and welcomes children. Telephone: 0136 782 0726.

- **HOW TO GET THERE:** Woolstone is 8 miles west of Wantage and 14 miles east of Swindon. It stands just off the B4507 road, that runs along the northern edge of the Lambourn Downs. The White Horse will be found at the northern end of the village.
- **PARKING:** There is a large pub car park, opposite the front entrance. Parking elsewhere in the village may be difficult, owing to the narrowness of the lanes. A public car park can be found south of the B4507, below Uffington Castle.
- **LENGTH OF THE WALK:** 5 miles. Map: OS Landranger 174 Newbury and Wantage (inn GR: 293877).

THE WALK

Turn left outside the White Horse to reach the next bend in the road. At this point, close to Upper Farm, a footpath signpost points the way ahead. Follow the direction indicated, taking the trackway to a stile and open farmland. The route is, in fact, quite clear. Keeping the hedgerow to your left, walk along the edges of two large fields, passing through a pedestrian gate on your way. Beyond the next stile you join another path that runs down through a belt of trees. Cross this path (turning left and immediately right) to emerge on the far side. Now you continue in the same direction (westwards) along more field edges, this time accompanying a wire fence. Through two metal farm gates, beside a line

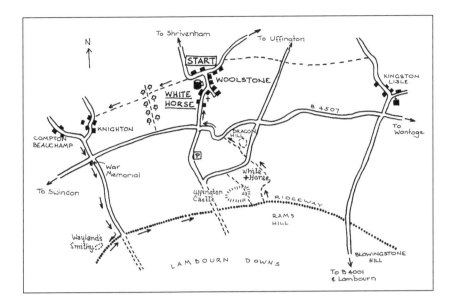

of trees and over a wooden plank bridge you will eventually meet the road at Knighton. Two final stiles will take you onto the tarmac. Turn left to walk through the hamlet, along a lane which curves its way past some thatched cottages. At the next junction, close to a large weather-boarded and thatched barn, turn left to reach the B4507 road.

Up to this point the views have been good – north across the Vale of the White Horse and south to the steep slopes of the Lambourn Downs. You may already have seen, upon the latter, the dragon-like shape of the White Horse. But now, from this road junction onwards, the views will get even better. As you gain height so look around. On clear days you can see the Cotswolds.

Before taking the long, steady climb up the lane opposite notice the little stone memorial which commemorates those locals who lost their lives in the Great War. Wreaths and garlands often decorate the spot.

The walk up the lane to the Ridgeway is about a mile long, but there is little traffic for the road is a dead end. When it reaches the Ridgeway the tarmac ends.

Before walking east to Uffington Castle and the White Horse you must first turn right (west) to visit Wayland's Smithy. This Stone Age burial chamber is some 5,000 years old. An information board tells its story. The present name comes from a Saxon legend that this was the forge of the god who shod the Uffington White Horse.

The walk along the Ridgeway is very easy, the trackway here being wide and firmly surfaced. It undulates somewhat but should not cause any difficulty. Uffington Castle - a Celtic hill fort - should soon be reached. The entire hilltop, including the White Horse and nearby Dragon Hill, is now owned by the National Trust. Visitors, therefore, can wander around almost at will. It is not known for sure when the White Horse was cut. It could be contemporary with the castle (Iron Age), but some say it is early Saxon. Interestingly it is best seen from above, although the view from the valley below is impressive enough.

The way back to Woolstone can be made most easily down the road that descends to the west of the castle, from the visitor car park. But the prettier and more interesting route for walkers is by footpath. This leaves the Ridgeway east of Uffington Castle, where a directional signpost points to a stile. Beyond this a grassy path runs alongside a wire fence and down the escarpment. As the gradient steepens this path bends right then left, and then narrows to follow an earthy gulley downhill. Crossing a country lane, the track continues, skirting round Dragon Hill and descending at an angle to the B4507 road. According to legend Dragon Hill is the site where St George slew the dragon. It is said that where the blood spilled on top of the mound, nothing now grows. At the road turn left to reach the next junction and then right to reach Woolstone.

 Ridgeway - Uffington White Horse to Blowingstone Hill (1½ miles)

The Ridgeway path continues eastward from the White Horse as a very clear, chalky track. It runs across Rams Hill, keeping to the edge of the Downs. Those wishing to walk this section can return to Woolstone via Kingston Lisle and a footpath across the meadows.

SPARSHOLT
The Star Inn

*T*his is a walk of sweeping views towards Oxford and the upper Thames valley. The outward route uses footpaths to reach the interesting village of Kingston Lisle, across the meadows, and then a country lane to reach the top of Blowingstone Hill. The return route is deep in horseracing country, by country lane down a chalk escarpment. The way is well marked throughout. The Ridgeway section included in this circular walk is from Blowingstone Hill to Hackpen Hill, a distance of 1½ miles.

Sparsholt boasts a number of thatched, half-timbered cottages, a Georgian manor house set in pretty landscaped grounds, and a large Gothic church full of carved woodwork, memorial brasses and medieval stained glass. In short, this is everyone's ideal of an English village.

The Star Inn is suitably traditional. It is 400 years old, contains low ceiling beams hung with tankards and has walls decorated with pictures, plates, guns and ornaments. The main bar room is long and narrow with the 'public' space at one end and the 'lounge' at the other. The atmosphere is comfortably cosy, the welcome is genuinely friendly. This is a freehouse serving a wide range of real ales, including Morland Original and two guest beers. Scrumpy Jack cider is on draught and the wines come from the four corners of Europe. The menu offers a wide choice, in bar snacks and main meals, and a blackboard lists daily specials. There are jacket potatoes, sandwiches and baguettes, all with various fillings; there are grills, steaks, chicken dishes and pies, all served with fresh vegetables; there are fish courses (like salmon and trout) and vegetarian meals (like cauliflower and leek with cheese sauce). The desserts include deep-dish apple pie, spotted dick and treacle sponge, these served with custard.

Normal pub opening times are kept and, not surprisingly, the place can sometimes be very busy. Telephone: 01235 751539.

• **HOW TO GET THERE:** Sparsholt is 4 miles west of Wantage and 18 miles east of Swindon. It stands just off the B4507 road and close to the B4001 that comes north from Lambourn. The Star Inn is in Watery Lane, at the northern end of the village.

• **PARKING:** The pub has its own car park but vehicles can also be left along the roadsides of the village. The lanes here are wide and not very busy.

• **LENGTH OF THE WALK:** 6 miles. Map: OS Landranger 174 Newbury and Wantage (inn GR: 347877).

THE WALK

Walk down the lane opposite the Star Inn (West Street) to the far end. There, pointing across the open field ahead, is a two-armed footpath signpost. One arm points half left, the other half right. Follow the former and head diagonally across to the far side aiming to the right of a line of tall trees. There you will find a track leading down beside a chalet bungalow. This takes you to a road, at the edge of Westcot village. Cross over this road and continue across the farmland on the other side. The direction to Kingston Lisle is indicated by a footpath signpost.

The way is very clear. Cross the first, very large, field by walking up to the skyline and down the other side of the hill, passing a lone telegraph pole on your way. Then, by joining a farm track, curve down into the bottom of a shallow valley. Across the stream an arrow disc points along a field edge, up a path that runs beside a belt of trees. At the top of this stretch, in due course, you reach the road at the northern edge of Kingston Lisle. Here turn left to walk through the village,

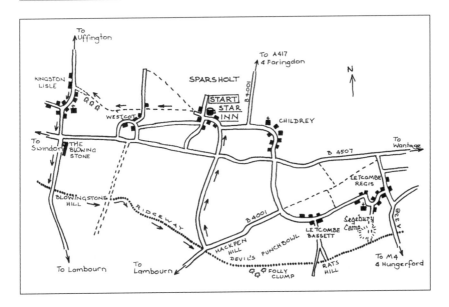

keeping left again beyond the church. This will bring you up to the B4507 road.

But hurry not through Kingston Lisle. Linger to admire the old cottages and stop to look at the 14th-century church, which contains some fine wall paintings. The nearby Kingston Lisle House, with its park and gardens, is open to the public and will certainly repay a later visit. The pub in the village is called the Blowing Stone Inn and Blowingstone Hill overlooks the surrounding countryside. You will find the origin of this name now standing in front of the row of cottages which you walk past, having just crossed the B4507 to begin the steep climb up to the Ridgeway. This is the Blowing Stone itself – a boulder of red sarsen perforated with little holes. Legend says that King Alfred used this stone to call his troops to battle. If blown correctly the stone holes produce a trumpet-like sound.

The Ridgeway path is reached soon after the steep gradient has levelled, close to a corrugated iron barn. Turn left to walk eastwards on this clear, gravel-rutted trackway. On the left are views across the Vale of the White Horse and over to the Didcot power station, to the right are the sweeping grasslands of the Lambourn Downs. Close at hand, also to the right, are some horse gallops. Ignoring the track that runs across to the left (this going down to Westcot) continue along the Ridgeway all the way to the road junction, close to which is a telegraph

The blowing stone in nearby Kingston Lisle

radio station. The B4001 crosses the track here. On the far side is Hackpen Hill, from where you can look down into the deep combe called Devil's Punchbowl.

The way back to Sparsholt is easy. Take the lane signposted, running steeply downhill to the B4507. Cross straight over this road to reach the Star Inn.

 RIDGEWAY - HACKPEN HILL TO SEGSBURY CAMP (3 MILES)

The Ridgeway path continues eastward from Hackpen Hill, in a long curve across the Downs. It is clear and firm underfoot. On the way it passes Folly Clump, a copse of beech trees, and crosses the summit of Rats Hill. Energetic walkers who wish to follow this section can return to Sparsholt via Letcombe Regis and Childrey.

LETCOMBE REGIS
The Greyhound

*O*n *its outward route this pleasant walk takes you through the heart of Iron Age Segsbury Camp. The return route uses bridleways and clear gravel tracks. The way is clear and firm underfoot throughout and the views are spectacular. The Ridgeway section included is from Segsbury Camp to Lord Wantage's Monument, a distance of 3 miles.*

Both Letcombe Regis and Letcombe Bassett are pretty, unspoilt villages with many ancient buildings. The former is the larger of the two, its name deriving from Crown ownership of the estate in Norman times. The latter was Thomas Hardy's model for the village of Cresscombe in his book *Jude the Obscure*. The meadows hereabouts have long been famous for their watercress-beds, which are fed by the clear spring waters emanating from the chalk downlands.

The Greyhound is a traditional village pub which has kept its friendly and unpretentious character. Inside there are two main rooms, one being a spacious public bar with pool table and wooden bench seats, the other being a cosy lounge with wall plates and brassware. Adjoining the latter there is also a small dining area. Outside is a pleasant beer garden with a children's play area.

This is a Morland house so the real ales served, such as Old Speckled Hen, come from that local brewery but other guest beers are also available, like Adnams Broadside. The draught cider is Scrumpy Jack and a small, but good selection of wines is available. All the food is well prepared and reasonably priced. Snacks range from sandwiches, filled rolls, ploughman's lunches and jacket potatoes; main meals include various meat and fish dishes. There are several curry options and a wide choice of vegetarian meals, including broccoli and nut bake, sweet-and-sour vegetables and lasagne.

The Greyhound opens all day, 11.30 am to 11 pm, and so is also convenient for afternoon teas. Telephone: 01235 770905.

- **HOW TO GET THERE:** Letcombe Regis is just 2 miles south-west of Wantage, nestling in the shadow of the Lambourn Downs. It is close to the A338 road to Hungerford and the B4507 road to Ashbury and Swindon. The Greyhound stands in the village centre, east of the church.
- **PARKING:** There is a large pub car park. Vehicles can also be left along the village streets where space permits. The lane leaving the village for the Downs is especially quiet, this being a cul-de-sac.
- **LENGTH OF THE WALK:** 7½ miles. Map: OS Landranger 174 Newbury and Wantage (inn GR: 382865). It should be noted that shorter sections of the Ridgeway can be walked using Letcombe Regis as a base, and shorter circuits can be devised. There are many roads and tracks leading up to the top of the Downs and these may be used by those wishing to curtail the circular walk described here.

The Walk

Turn left outside the Greyhound and left again at the church. Round the top corner is the Sparrow public house, also to be recommended. This lane is a no-through road and leads directly to the downland escarpment. Follow it all the way to the point where it joins the Ridgeway path, which is little more than a mile away. This is an extremely pleasant walk, with hedges either side and views to the right across the meadows to Hackpen Hill. As the road climbs Castle Hill, stiles on each side lead into pastures which have been given 'access land' status. Visitors can wander at will over the hillside and inspect, at close

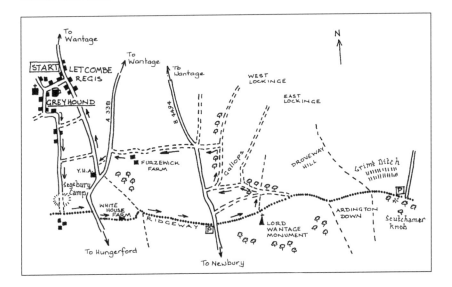

quarters, the Iron Age hill-fort called Segsbury Camp. Covering an enormous 26 acres, the earthworks were once faced with sarsen stones, some of which can still be seen.

The lane becomes a gravel track as it cuts through the centre of Segsbury Camp, before meeting the Ridgeway on the far side, close to a farmstead. Turn left to follow the Ridgeway path eastwards. Here the National Trail is a wide, fenced gravel trackway popular with cyclists and horseriders. Unusually, the views are southwards across the sweep of the chalky Berkshire Downs and not northwards. This is because the land rises slightly to the left, the track being lower than the ridgetop.

The Ridgeway crosses the main A338 road going right then left, and continues past White House Farm. Thereafter it bends sharp left to reach a junction of bridleways. Those wishing to shorten the walk can turn left here, following the sign to Court Hill Ridgeway Centre. Otherwise the Ridgeway should be followed to the right. Along this next stretch the way is a wide grassy ride, rutted by vehicles. Ahead you will see the radio mast at Betterton Down and now, you will see the view to the left over Didcot Power Station. Lord Wantage's Monument will soon be reached, on the far side of the B4494. This commemorates Baron Wantage of Lockinge who was not only a war hero of the Crimea but also a great and philanthropic local landowner.

The way back to Letcombe Regis begins downhill from the Monument following the signposted direction to a small woodland. Just

41

before the trees, cross over a gravel track and bear left down another wide lane. A sign states 'Farm Vehicles Only' but this is a public bridleway. Later, where this lane turns right continue straight on along a grassy track, an arrow disc pointing the way. To the right along here is an area given over to horse gallops. Shortly before the B4494 road turn right (keeping the gallops alongside) and continue northwards past a coniferous wood. Shortly after this turn left, along a wide earth-beaten track. This leads across the B4494 and westwards for another mile to reach the A338. All the while are views to the right, so this stretch should not be rushed. To the left are the Downs – high, green and steep. Upon reaching the A338 turn left, uphill, and then after 200 yards right through a farm gate. Crossing the field diagonally you soon reach a lane. Close by is the Court Hill Ridgeway Centre and Youth Hostel. Turn right. This quiet lane will lead you downhill all the way back to Letcombe Regis.

 ### RIDGEWAY - LORD WANTAGE'S MONUMENT TO SCUTCHAMER KNOB (2½ MILES)

The Ridgeway along this stretch is a very wide, grassy much-rutted trackway with spectacular views northwards. Ardington Down, over which the National Trail runs, rises to nearly 700 ft above sea level. On the lower slopes of that downland is a section of Grim's Ditch, a prehistoric earthwork that once helped defend the Vale of the White Horse.

WEST ILSLEY

The Harrow

This elevated walk offers a beautiful panorama from the downland ridge and an exciting glimpse into the world of the modern racehorse. Both the outward and the return routes follow clear trackways, and the going is firm and dry. The views to be enjoyed across the upper Thames valley are superb. The Ridgeway section included in this circular walk is from Scutchamer Knob to Gore Hill, a distance of 2½ miles.

The villages of East and West Ilsley are famous as centres for racehorse training, and the downlands all around have areas set aside for gallops. The turf here is specially managed to provide a thick mat of springy grass. East Ilsley, the larger of the two villages, was home to a large medieval sheep fair in the heyday of England's wool trade.

The Harrow stands opposite the village pond and cricket pitch. It is suitably old, traditional and friendly. Inside there are low ceiling beams, stone fireplaces, Victorian prints decorating the dark walls and well-worn antique furniture. The single bar room is separated into two sections, one being a no-smoking dining area.

But it is not the age and decor of this pub that makes the place unique, it is the food on offer. There is a standard menu and several blackboards list the many daily specials, but always the dishes are wholesome, hearty and home-made. Meat pies and traditional English puddings are a speciality whilst a selection of unusual British farmhouse cheeses is always available. These are sold off-sales and, indeed, by mail order. Bar snacks include granary rolls, with various fillings, salads, soups and ploughman's lunches. Main dishes include such tempting items as lamb and apricot pie, home-made sausages, and chicken with mushrooms and cream. Salmon, trout and halibut feature on the menus regularly and vegetarians can enjoy such dishes as courgette and hazelnut bake, lentil patties with tomato sauce and a 'pasta of the day'.

The Harrow is a Morland pub and therefore serves a full range of real ales, produced by the Abingdon-based brewery, like Original and Bill's Spring Brew. There is also a guest beer like Flowers Original. Gaymers Old English cider and a full wine selection are also on offer. Normal pub opening times are kept, families are welcome and there is children's play equipment in the garden. Telephone: 01635 281260.

- **HOW TO GET THERE:** West Ilsley is 5 miles south-east of Wantage and 10 miles north of Newbury. It is just off the busy A34 trunk road. The Harrow stands at the western end of the village.
- **PARKING:** There is a pub car park, but vehicles can easily be left elsewhere in the village, since the roads are wide and quiet. Gravel parking areas are provided next to the village pond and close to the footpath at the start of the circular walk.
- **LENGTH OF THE WALK:** 5½ miles. Map: OS Landranger 174 Newbury and Wantage (inn GR: 470827).

THE WALK

The path that leads up to the Ridgeway begins just a few yards west of the Harrow, so turn right as you leave the main entrance. A signpost points the way, up a wide gravel track. This is, in fact, a bridleway and is marked, upon later signs, by a blue arrow. Do be aware of horse traffic as you walk – racehorses are sensitive animals. Keep to this track all the way, for a distance of 1½ miles, ignoring other paths and tracks that lead off to the right. The route is very clear, alongside a wire fence. To the left is the Hendred Estate farmland, and a view across the rolling

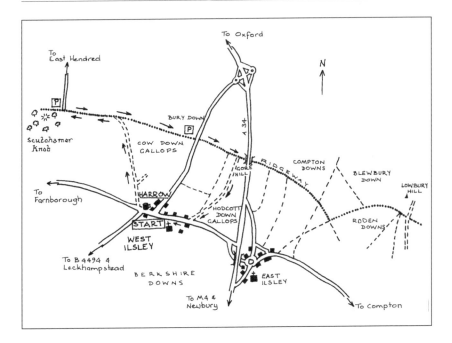

Berkshire Downs. To the right are the Cow Down Racehorse Gallops. The song of skylarks may be heard above your head, or the call of curlews. A splendid walk this, and one that should be savoured.

In due course you reach the top, the steady ascent culminating in a view northwards across the Vale of the White Horse. Here you join the Ridgeway, at an angle. Continue straight on (westwards) to reach Scutchamer Knob, just ¼ mile away.

Set amidst the trees of a small hilltop wood, Scutchamer Knob will be found close to the place where the lane to East Hendred village begins. There are car parking spaces here for those who drive to visit this ancient site. The Knob is a large burial mound, thought to be Bronze Age in origin. Now just 15 ft high and horseshoe in shape it was once much more impressive. Sadly the place was devastated by Victorian archaeologists, who found just a few fragments of Celtic pottery and an iron buckle. Legend says that Scutchamer was the burial place of the Saxon King Cwichelm of Wessex, who died in AD 593.

Retrace your steps to continue the walk eastwards along the Ridgeway. This section from Scutchamer Knob to Gore Hill offers some of the finest views in southern England. The downland ridge here is some 600 ft above sea level and the panorama on clear days is superb.

45

To the left is a sweep of distant hills, forward across the Thames valley to the Chilterns, back across the Vale of Oxford to the Cotswolds. Even the Didcot Power Station and the Harwell Research Establishment, down below, detract little from the spectacle.

The Ridgeway path along this stretch is over 50 ft wide, part of which is gravel, part grassland. It is also one of the most popular sections for all forms of traffic. So walkers must share the way with horse-riders, cyclists, farmers, motor bike riders and even 4 x 4 car enthusiasts. Even so, the walk is immensely enjoyable.

Gore Hill is reached about half a mile beyond the Bury Down car park (the car park being where the lane to West Ilsley crosses the Ridgeway). The A34 dual carriageway runs close by. In the days of horse and coach traffic, Gore Hill was a notorious spot for winter travellers, who frequently became snow-bound here.

The way back to West Ilsley begins at the top of Gore Hill, down a gravel track heading south. From Bury Down this is the second signposted route on the right-hand side, the first being a bridleway that runs along a field edge. The way to follow is marked as a 'road used as public path' and runs downhill beside some racehorse gallops (which are on your left). This gravel track descends steadily, beside a woodland, eventually to reach the eastern end of West Ilsley village. At the road turn right to return to the Harrow.

 ### RIDGEWAY - GORE HILL TO LOWBURY HILL (4 MILES)

The Ridgeway path continues eastwards from Gore Hill across a number of racehorse gallops. After passing under the A34 it veers south-eastwards over Compton Downs and then north-eastwards over Roden Downs. All the way it is extremely clear and firm underfoot. North of Compton the Ridgeway crosses the line of the Old Didcot, Newbury and Southampton Joint Railway. This was opened in 1882 and closed in the 1960s. Walkers can return to West Ilsley from Lowbury Hill via East Ilsley, a most attractive village.

ALDWORTH
The Bell Inn
❧

*W**alkers should take their time to enjoy this circuit, for the views are wide and the wildlife varied. The outward route is by country lane and trackway, the return route is by clear bridleway. The Ridgeway section included in this circular walk is from Lowbury Hill which, it is said, commands one of the finest views from the National Trail, to Thurle Down, a distance of 2½ miles.*

Aldworth is a small, rather isolated village set high on the Berkshire Downs. Yet it is fairly well-known. This is partly because of its ancient church, with its large old yew tree outside and 14th-century carved effigies inside; partly because of the village well, at 372 ft one of the deepest in England; and partly because it boasts two excellent pubs. The Four Points, at the southern end, is thatched and homely; the Bell Inn at the northern end, is even older and even more original. Both can be highly recommended.

Thought to date from 1340, the Bell occupies a 'cruck' type of manor or 'hall' house. Inside, the atmosphere is totally traditional. The rooms are small, dark, low-beamed and cosy, the walls are plastered and wood-planked, and the bar counter is a glass-panelled hatch. There are two rooms – the smoke room and tap room. In one of these are pub games, in the other are a couple of fascinating brick alcoves. In the recent past the Bell has won the 'Unspoilt Pub of the Year' award, and how richly deserved! No wonder the place gets packed at weekends.

Various real ales are offered, since this is a freehouse. These include Arkell's and Morrells beers (like 3B, Kingsdown and Oxford Bitter) together with some local brews. Bulmers cider and selected wines are also served. The food is plain and simple, wholesome and excellent value. Hot crusty rolls, with various fillings, are the speciality of the house, whilst hearty soups are available in winter. Puddings like hot chocolate sponge and treacle sponge will fill the most cavernous of stomachs. The Bell Inn keeps normal pub opening times but closes Monday lunchtimes. Families are welcome, there is a very pleasant garden, and everyone will be assured a most pleasant experience. Telephone: 01635 578272.

- **HOW TO GET THERE:** Aldworth is 10 miles north-east of Newbury and 10 miles north-west of Reading. It stands just 3 miles west of the river Thames at Goring, on the B4009 road from Streatley. The Bell will be found north of the church.
- **PARKING:** There is a pub car park but this can easily become full. Vehicles can be left along the surrounding lanes, which are quiet, provided no obstruction is caused.
- **LENGTH OF THE WALK:** 6½ miles. Map: OS Landranger 174 Newbury and Wantage (inn GR: 556797). It should be noted that the circuit can be shortened by omitting Lowbury Hill and walking along the Ridgeway for just 2 miles.

The Walk

Turn right outside the Bell Inn and walk up the lane signposted to 'The Downs'. This is a dead-end thoroughfare so there should be very little passing traffic. Simply enjoy the widening views as you make your long, slow ascent to the Ridgeway path, which is 2 miles away.

Ignoring paths and bridleways on either side continue along the tarmac road all the way to the farmstead of Starveall. Beyond this, a wide gravel track continues in the same direction, indicated by a red arrow on

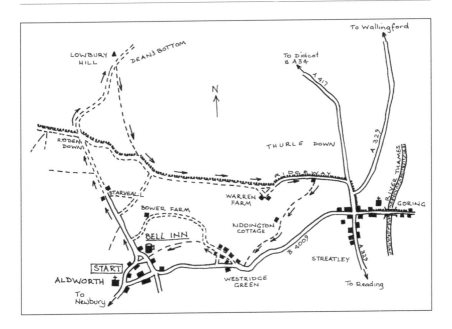

a signpost. Follow this, once again ignoring paths leading off on either side. Very soon you join the Ridgeway, which you meet at an angle. Here you could turn right and immediately head eastwards along the Ridgeway path but a detour to Lowbury Hill would repay the effort. Accordingly cross over the Ridgeway and follow the trackway opposite. This bends right to climb the quarter of a mile to the Lowbury summit.

At the top, looking north beyond the Didcot Power Station you will see Oxford; east beyond the Thames are the Chiltern Hills. Turn round and look southwards. On clear days you can see the blue line of the North Downs around the Basingstoke area. West are the racehorse gallops of Compton Downs and east, down below, is the deep little combe called Dean's Bottom. Lowbury Hill must have been an important stronghold once. Iron Age burial mounds scatter the area and the site of a 4th-century Roman encampment has been discovered near the summit, together with the remains of a Roman temple.

You can return to the Ridgeway path either by retracing your steps down the trackway or by following the clear footpath that heads south-east, diagonally across a field. The Ridgeway eastwards from Lowbury is a byway, that is a clear trackway running between fields and hedgerows. Other tracks lead off on either side but the route is obvious. In front is Thurle Down, the landscape dipping towards the river Thames. In due

49

course, beyond Warren Farm, the Ridgeway becomes tarmac-surfaced and the countryside around becomes more timbered. Warren Farm itself is now run by the Kulika Charitable Trust, which encourages sustainable agriculture in Africa. Organic produce is often on sale here: enquire at the barn.

The return to Aldworth begins at Wynders, a house which stands half a mile east of Warren Farm. Turn right here along a gravel-and-grass trackway signposted as a footpath. The way is very pretty. Beyond the first hedgerows and trees the track strikes across open farmland, along the bottom of a shallow valley. In due course it winds past Kiddington Cottage and climbs along the top edge of a small woodland. At the top it meets the B4009 road at Westridge Green. At this point you turn right.

To return to the Bell Inn you could stay on the road and turn right at the next junction. But a more pleasant route lies across the farmland. Beyond Westridge Green, where the road bends left, continue up the gravel track straight on. Past the last of the houses this track bends right. At this point turn left. A very clear footpath now leads across two fields, to emerge at Aldworth, beside the Bell Inn garden.

 ### RIDGEWAY - THURLE DOWN TO THE RIVER THAMES (1½ MILES)

From Thurle Down the Ridgeway follows a country lane eastwards, down to the A417. From there it accompanies main roads to the river Thames, via Streatley to Goring. Streatley is a pretty riverside village with many 18th-century buildings. The grassy hillslopes that rise up either side of the B4009 road are owned by the National Trust. From these, superb views may be enjoyed across the gorge-like Goring Gap.

GORING
The Catherine Wheel

In contrast with all other sections walked in this book, the Ridgeway here is 'civilised' - instead of crossing chalk uplands with wide views it follows a riverbank track beside meadows and manicured gardens. The prospect is intimate and charming. The return route follows clear trackways and paths across open farmland and through pretty woods with the way clear throughout. The Ridgeway section included in this circular walk is along the river Thames from Goring to South Stoke, a distance of 2 miles.

Goring-on-Thames, as it is sometimes called, is a village with the bustle of a small town. It is an attractive place with a mix of building styles and a number of winding lanes. The bridge and riverside walk offer pretty views along the Thames and the medieval church contains embellished roof timbers and a 600 year old bell. For thirsty travellers there are tea shops and several pubs. Amongst the latter the Catherine Wheel is the oldest.

The pub's dark, cosy interior does not disappoint the expectant customer. Several small rooms, some at different levels and one with a tiled floor, are decorated and furnished in rustic and traditional fashion. The dining room alongside was once an old forge. Low ceiling beams, wood panelled walls and bottle-filled plate shelves offer a welcome which is matched by the friendly staff. This is very much a 'local' for the walls are covered with notices and posters announcing all manner of events, clubs and village information.

This being a Brakspear pub, the real ales offered include OBJ, Mild, Special and Old. The draught cider is Strongbow and the wine list is wide and reasonably priced. The food served is excellent, from snacks like rolls, jacket potatoes and salads to main meals like steaks, meat pies and various fish dishes. The regular menu is supplemented by daily specials chalked up on the blackboard and these may include, in season, local asparagus, trout and salmon. There are vegetable and pasta bakes and desserts include such items as chocolate fudge cake and apple crumble. The Catherine Wheel keeps normal pub opening times. Telephone: 01491 872379.

- **HOW TO GET THERE:** Goring is 8 miles south-east of Didcot and 9 miles north-west of the centre of Reading. The A329 Wallingford to Pangbourne road runs through Streatley which is Goring's neighbour across the Thames. Goring itself stands on the B4009. The Catherine Wheel will be found south of the High Street, along Manor Road.
- **PARKING:** There is no pub car park but a large public car park can be found immediately behind the Catherine Wheel. Here and there parking is also allowed along the back lanes of the village, provided no obstruction is caused.
- **LENGTH OF THE WALK:** 5 miles. Maps: OS Landranger 174 Newbury and Wantage, 175 Reading and Windsor (inn GR: 600806). This walk crosses the edge between two OS Maps.

THE WALK

Outside the Catherine Wheel turn right. This road curves round and will take you to the bottom of Goring High Street. On the way it passes the John Barleycorn pub, another establishment that can be recommended with confidence. Turn left at the High Street to reach the bridge across the river Thames. Those with time should stop awhile. There are views in both directions, upstream to the weir and Goring Lock, downstream across the meadows. Many boats are moored here and trips can be

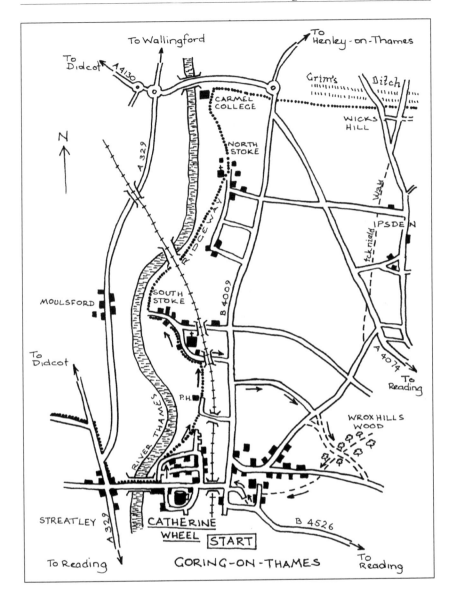

arranged. The nearby church should also be visited.

The Ridgeway path leaves the High Street just a few yards from the bridge, down Thames Road. A signpost marks the way. At the far end (this being a cul-de-sac), a tarmac path continues in the same direction. This runs between hedges, fences and walls, for there are

Goring lock

gardens and houses either side. At the next road, which you join opposite Clevemede, turn left to walk downhill past a small housing estate. Towards the bottom you pass some handsome old houses, including Cleve Mill. Beyond these the road ends but the Ridgeway path continues as a gravel bridleway. This next section is also signposted as the Swans Way. This is a designated long distance bridle route from Goring to Salcey Forest in northern Buckinghamshire, a distance of 65 miles.

The way is clearly marked, so a detailed description is not necessary. Between hedges and fences the path runs below lines of trees. Down to the left are glimpses of the river, to the right is the embanked railway line carrying inter-city trains. Emerging onto a lane, continue in the same direction, keeping the Leatherne Bottle pub down to your left (unless of course, a thirst-quenching detour is required). The 'Private Road', crossed by ramps, is signposted as the Ridgeway and this provides an attractive stretch. To the right are large detached residences with gardens to admire, to the left are lawns sloping down to the riverside. In due course this road ends and the Ridgeway path continues across a couple of fields to South Stoke. At the road you can either turn right, to shorten the circuit a little, or left to look at the village centre. The latter is recommended. Here you will find a number of old farms (including Manor Farm, which boasts the second largest dovecote in England), a pretty Gothic church and the hospitable Perch and Pike Inn.

The return to Goring begins along the B4009 which runs down the eastern edge of the village. About 500 yards south of the village's southern end turn left along a lane marked as a single track road. Beyond the attractive Grove Farm you reach a T-junction. Turn right and then, almost immediately left, along a grassy track that curves alongside a hedgerow. Close to an electricity sub-station you join a wider track and turn left. Up to this point the scenery, though pretty, has been rather treeless. But now this is about to change, for ahead lies Wroxhills Wood.

Follow the track all the way to the edge of this woodland, where a bridleway signpost points the way to Elvendon. Follow the grassy track indicated as it curves beneath the trees. What a pleasant stretch this is! After about 400 yards you leave the Elvendon-bound bridleway, to follow a narrower track - in fact a footpath - which curves off to the right. This bends a little and then descends along the outside edge of the woodland. The views to the right are towards Goring Gap and the grassy slopes above Streatley. At the bottom is a country lane. Almost opposite another footpath leads directly to Goring village. This runs beside some garden fences and then, beyond a stile, crosses the bottom corner of a field. Emerging onto a gravel lane, turn left to reach the B4526, and then, right. Now follow the signs to 'village via Farm Close'. Goring centre is reached across the railway bridge.

 ### RIDGEWAY - SOUTH STOKE TO WICKS HILL (4½ MILES)

From South Stoke the Ridgeway follows the river Thames all the way to Carmel College, at the southern edge of Wallingford. This is now a school, set amidst some attractive landscaped grounds. North Stoke, which is seen a mile before Carmel College, is a pretty village once the home of the opera singer Dame Clara Butt. Beyond Carmel College the Ridgeway turns east to make the long ascent up Wicks Hill along the line of Grim's Ditch.

IPSDEN

The King William IV

A walk in unspoilt countryside with, here and there, extensive views to be enjoyed. The outward route follows a clear track, whilst the return route follows a footpath across farmland and a pretty 'green road'. The Ridgeway section included in this circular walk is from Wicks Hill to Nuffield, a distance of 2 miles. This stretch follows the line of Grim's Ditch thought to be Iron Age and which was probably dug as a defensive boundary between tribal kingdoms. The section seen on this walk is especially clear.

Ipsden is not a large village, but it is spread out, being dispersed across the green fields of the southern Chilterns. It is also an attractive and interesting village. Ipsden Farm boasts the longest barn in Oxfordshire (dating from the 18th century), Well Place has a little zoo, and the Reade Memorial is linked to a curious ghost story; involving an appearance of a man who had died in India. And at Hailey, on the northern edge of

Ipsden, is one of the best and most traditional pubs in this part of England.

The King William IV is mentioned in many a pub guide and walking book, and well it might be. The building dates back to Tudor times and has kept its rustic character beautifully. Inside all is dark with low, oak beams, and bare stone and brick walls. Old farm implements hang from hooks and a log fire burns in the grate whenever the weather turns chilly. Locals pin their cards and posters around the bar – for the place is truly a village 'local'. The single bar room has three sections, one end being a lounge type area. Outside the lawns are covered with more country artifacts – old ploughs, root cutters and so on – whilst the landlord keeps a pedigree shire horse in a nearby paddock.

This is a Brakspear house and the ales are served straight from the barrels: pale and mild, 4X and Old. There is scrumpy cider (also from a barrel) and wines are sold by the glass. Food is plain and simple: ploughman's and filled rolls (various fillings), home-made soups and pies. Excellent value and very enjoyable, these should be sampled. Normal pub opening times are kept. Telephone: 01491 680675.

- **HOW TO GET THERE:** Ipsden is 8 miles west of Henley-on-Thames, just to the east of the A4074 Reading to Wallingford road. The hamlet of Hailey, where stands the King William IV, will be found along a cul-de-sac at the northern end of Ipsden.
- **PARKING:** There is a large pub car park. Vehicles can also be left in the nearby laybys, where space permits.
- **LENGTH OF THE WALK:** 6 miles. Map: OS Landranger 175 Reading and Windsor (inn GR: 642858).

THE WALK

Outside the King William IV turn right and then, very soon, right again. Next to Stone Farm a clear trackway is signposted as a footpath. At first the surface is rough tarmac but soon this degenerates into gravel and grass. It is wide, clear and firm nevertheless and heads northwards in a fairly straight line. Beyond the Poors Farm buildings continue up alongside a small woodland, which is on your left. Soon a grassy track leads off on the right. Ignore this and go straight on, following a tractor-rutted way across a field. On the far side is Wicks Wood. Over an old cattle-grid you enter this woodland and follow the main track that continues under the trees. This curves left and descends to Woodhouse Farm, where you meet a gravel farm track. Turn left.

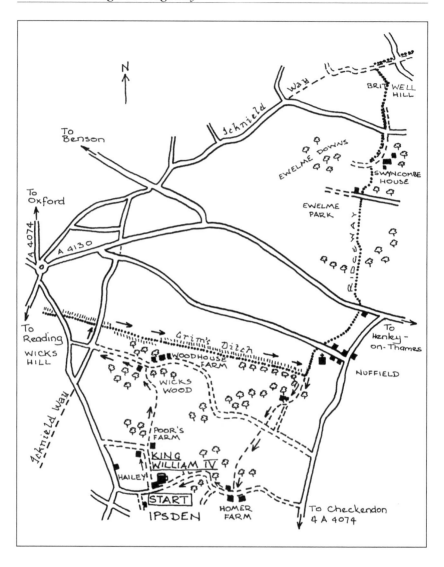

So far the countryside has been pretty, unspoilt and varied. Walkers are thus advised to take their time. From the open hill country, from where there are views left towards Didcot Power Station, you enter a charming deciduous woodland where much replanting has been done recently. Wildlife is abundant and you would be unlucky not to see rabbits, squirrels and pheasants.

West of Woodhouse Farm you soon join a country lane, where you turn right. This lane, incidentally, follows the line of the prehistoric Icknield Way, the Celtic trade route that linked the old Ridgeway at the Thames at Goring with the North Sea coast, following the chalk escarpments of the Chilterns and East Anglian Heights. You follow this Icknield route for only about 500 yards, for at the foot of Wicks Hill you will meet the Ridgeway National Trail.

The Ridgeway Path crosses the old Icknield Way along the line of Grim's Ditch. Down from the left it has descended Wicks Hill as a bridleway; up to the right it continues as a footpath. Follow the latter direction. The grassy track follows the edge of a field, curves round a woodland and continues eastward in an almost straight line. The belt of trees and bushes it follows marks the line of Grim's Ditch, two embankments enclosing a central dyke. Considering its great age this is truly impressive, the slopes still being steep. In Celtic times this must surely have been an important boundary.

The Ridgeway rises and falls with the contours of the landscape and the views either side are across undulating chalk downlands. Behind are the towers of Didcot Power Station, with the Vale of Oxford beyond. In due course the field edge track becomes indistinct. Fear not. The Ridgeway path now enters the wooded belt and follows the line of the embankments. The way is clear as it proceeds beneath the trees, first along one embankment, then the other, then along the first one again. At some points you need to cross over stiles, at other points through kissing gates. Eventually, beyond a white-painted house, Grim's Ditch suddenly ends and a choice presents itself. To the left the Ridgeway continues into Nuffield village. To the right is a footpath. Follow the latter direction.

The way back is clear enough. Over a stile the footpath runs south through and along a belt of trees. Notice, along this stretch, the views to the right, to the Oxfordshire Plain beyond Didcot. Beyond the trees, the path continues along a field edge, over a metal ladder stile and through a thicket. It then bends round the edge of private grounds to emerge onto a private drive. Go straight over, then bear left down a grassy track to reach the road at a T-junction. A right-of-way almost opposite crosses a large field, curves round a woodland copse and meets a 'green road' at Homer Farm. Turn right. This 'green road' is a gravel track unused by vehicular traffic. It winds under the trees, skirts a woodland and offers splendid views either side. Keeping right at the first junction, left at the second, you will eventually reach the King William IV.

The village well at Ipsden

 RIDGEWAY - NUFFIELD TO BRITWELL HILL (4½ MILES)

From Nuffield the Ridgeway Route is slightly complicated, winding somewhat between villages. However, it is clearly signposted throughout. North of the A4130 (where stands the Crown Inn) it passes Ewelme Park and Swyncombe House. The countryside is well timbered here and so the views are intimate and leafy. Close to Britwell Hill the Ridgeway National Trail rejoins the route of the old Icknield Way.

WATLINGTON
The Fox and Hounds

A pleasant walk in pretty countryside with optional detours to the top of the Chiltern ridge, which is attractively wooded. From there the panorama is worth the effort of the climb. The outward route is by footpath across farmland, the return is along a tarmac track which forms part of the Oxfordshire Way. The Ridgeway section included in this circular walk is from Britwell Hill to Pyrton Hill, a distance of 1½ miles. This stretch follows the line of the old Icknield Way which runs along the foot of the Chiltern escarpment.

Watlington is smaller than it appears, with its busy High Street, network of lanes and alleyways, and its grand 17th-century town hall. In June 1643 the Roundhead John Hampden spent the night here before the Battle of Chalgrove, during the English Civil War. At that battle, 3 miles north-west, he was mortally wounded. Today a monument marks the spot.

The Fox and Hounds reflects the character of Watlington, being a cosy town pub with traditionally rustic features. The one large bar room is subdivided, one end being unpretentiously decorated and furnished with pool table and television, the other end being comfortably fitted out as a lounge. There are low beams, open fires and an atmosphere worthy of a 17th-century hostelry. There is a restaurant here and bed and breakfast facilities are provided. Outside, at the rear, is a gravelled sitting area by the garden.

This Brakspear house sells Brakspear's Ordinary and Best Bitters, Strongbow draught cider and a good selection of wines. The food is good and reasonably priced. Bar snacks include filled granary rolls, ploughman's platters and steak-in-a-bun; main meals range from various items with chips (like meat pie, cod or turkey) to interesting vegetarian dishes (like tuna and pasta bake and Mediterranean filo parcels). There are also house specialities like lime and chilli chicken. The Fox and Hounds has normal pub opening times. Telephone: 01491 612142.

- **HOW TO GET THERE:** Watlington is 6 miles north-east of Wallingford and 12 miles west of High Wycombe. It stands on the B4009 road that runs along the foot of the Chiltern Hills. Junction 6 of the M40 motorway is only 3 miles away. The Fox and Hounds will be found on the B4009 at the eastern end of the village.
- **PARKING:** There is a large pub car park at the rear, reached alongside the building. Vehicles can also be left in many of the side streets nearby, notably in Love Lane just to the east.
- **LENGTH OF THE WALK:** 4½ miles. Map: OS Landranger 175 Reading and Windsor (inn GR: 690946).

THE WALK

Turn right outside the Fox and Hounds and walk through Watlington along the B4009 (here called Couching Street). At the far end is a T-junction. Turn right along the B480 in the direction of Oxford (Brook Road). There are some old cottages along here and these should be admired before turning left along the required footpath. This path will be found some 200 yards from the junction, marked by a yellow arrow disc fixed to a telegraph pole. It runs up beside an old cottage and then bends between garden walls. A stile leads into the open fields.

Cross the first field diagonally, half right, to a stile in the far corner, then left where the path forks. Continue along by a wire fence with the hedgerow on your left. Keep left at the wide gravel track which you

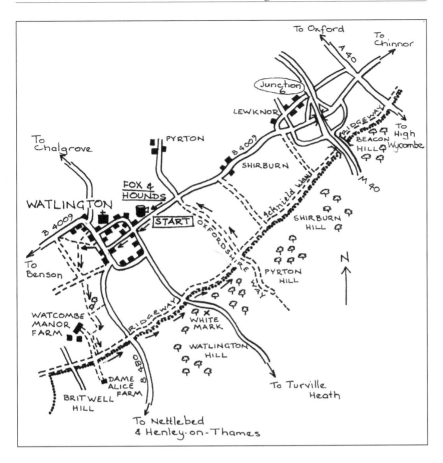

soon join. At the T-junction with another wide trackway cross over and follow a narrower path which curves uphill opposite. A painted arrow, on a nearby post, points the way. This path bends around a copse of trees, which encircles a pond, and proceeds across the farmland running between large open fields. Britwell Hill is now ahead and the line of the Chiltern escarpment stretches away to the left. Ignoring another footpath that joins from the left continue uphill, to follow the route as it turns right and eventually meets a concrete farm track. To the right is a cluster of agricultural buildings, which you avoid. Now turn left. Do not walk along the concrete track but follow the field edge path that runs parallel to it on the other side of the hedgerow. The Ridgeway will be reached beyond the far corner, over a stile. Britwell Hill is now immediately ahead and above. Turn left along the National Trail.

The Ridgeway path along here is concrete-surfaced since it is used by vehicles associated with the Watcombe Manor Farm workshop complex and by nearby Dame Alice Farm. Happily, it becomes a quieter gravel trackway again beyond the B480. Up to the right is the wooded Watlington Hill. This is owned by the National Trust and is protected as an area of Special Scientific Interest. Those wishing to explore the area can take one of the paths that lead uphill from the Ridgeway, access being permitted. On the slope facing Watlington village, and visible from the lane that crosses the Ridgeway, is the White Mark. This pyramid or spire-shaped chalk figure was cut in 1764, for reasons unknown. Half a mile beyond crossing the lane to Watlington you reach another junction. This time a trackway comes down from Pyrton Hill, to the right, and continues, tarmac-covered, down to the left.

The return to Watlington follows this tarmac track. It is part of the Oxfordshire Way, a long distance footpath 65 miles long, that links the Chilterns with the Cotswolds. Running from Henley-on-Thames to Bourton-on-the-Water it wanders attractively across the upper Thames valley. Where the Way crosses the B4009 turn left along that road to reach the Fox and Hounds. There is a pavement all the way.

RIDGEWAY - PYRTON HILL TO BEACON HILL (2½ MILES)

From the Oxfordshire Way, below Pyrton Hill, the Ridgeway continues as a clear, fenced trackway along the line of the old Icknield Way. It follows the bottom of the Chiltern escarpment and runs under the M40 motorway near Lewknor.

KINGSTON BLOUNT
The Cherry Tree
❧❀❧

T̲his enjoyable walk follows the line of the prehistoric Icknield Way, the Celtic trade route that linked the old Ridgeway with the North Sea coast. The old Way is followed, along a wide trackway which is firm underfoot and fenced either side. The outward route is by bridleway via Aston Rowant; the return route is by track via the hamlet of Crowell. The Ridgeway section included in this circular walk is from Beacon Hill to Crowell Hill, a distance of 1½ miles.

Within earshot of the M40, along the spring line below the Chiltern escarpment, stand three quiet villages. Lewknor has a Norman church and, at Moor Court, a fine 18th century manor house set within a medieval moat. Aston Rowant is dominated by two stud farms and Kingston Blount has a collection of old thatched cottages scattered around several farms. The last named village also boasts an excellent stopping and refreshment point, our featured pub, the Cherry Tree.

The Cherry Tree is not an especially old building but its atmosphere is wonderfully traditional. Beams, wooden bench seats and old sporting prints give the required character and, judging from the posters of local events which decorate the walls, the place is still very much the centre of village life. There is one main bar room at the front and a pool room at the rear.

The real ales served include Brakspear Bitter, and Marlow beers like Rebellion Mutiny and Rebellion Smugglers. The draught cider is Strongbow and Scrumpy Jack and a good, if limited, wine selection is available. The food served is well cooked and excellent value, the range being wholesome rather than haute cuisine. From all kinds of sandwiches and ploughman's lunches the menu rises through grills, pies, scampi and curry to lasagnes and pasta salads. Service is friendly and welcoming. Normal pub opening times are kept. Telephone: 01844 352273.

- **HOW TO GET THERE:** Kingston Blount is 5 miles south of Thame and 9 miles north-west of High Wycombe. It is 2 miles from Junction 6 on the M40, along the B4009 to Princes Risborough. The Cherry Tree stands on the B4009 at the southern edge of the village.
- **PARKING:** There is a pub car park. Vehicles can also be left along the village lanes, but not along the B4009 itself which can be busy.
- **LENGTH OF THE WALK:** 4½ miles. Map: OS Landranger 165 Aylesbury and Leighton Buzzard (inn GR: 739994). Those with time may like to extend the circuit by climbing Beacon Hill and exploring Aston Woods, through land owned by the National Trust and an area run as a nature reserve.

THE WALK

Walk west from the Cherry Tree along the B4009 and then turn right down the lane to Sydenham. This skirts the edge of the village and passes the signs that point up a track to the old Shoulder of Mutton pub. Opposite Brook Street turn left along a footpath signposted to Aston Rowant. This is a firm gravelled way that leads up and alongside a field. It is called the 'Moors Path' and is not, officially, a bridleway (although horses do use it). In due course this path runs alongside a cricket pitch, between wooden fences and hedges, and beside a village school. It emerges at Aston Rowant, where you continue beside a wall to reach the road. There a left turn will bring you up to the church, Aston House Stud and, eventually, the B4009. So far the Chiltern escarpment has been distant, to the left. Now, however, as you veer south, it is ahead and

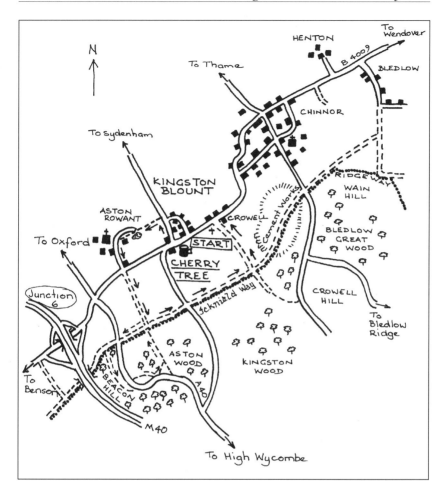

becoming ever closer. Across the B4009 follow the 'private road' past Woodway Farm, which is signposted as a bridleway. The Ridgeway path is soon reached, some little way before the ridge. Aston Wood is directly in front, Beacon Hill is up to the right.

● Unlike many other prehistoric trackways, the old Icknield Way did not follow the ridges or high levels. It kept largely to the spring line – the bottom of the hillslope where springs emerged to give water supply. Thus, the Ridgeway National Trail along this stretch maintains a level of just 400 ft, about half the height of the escarpment summits. The views to the north, therefore, are wide but not extensive. The upper Thames valley is seen as a low horizon. Those wanting to widen their view can take a 2 mile detour. A right turn will take them along the Ridgeway to the A40 and then a footpath can be followed up to the top of Beacon Hill. From there forest paths lead through Aston Rowant Nature Reserve, a return to the Ridgeway being possible down Kingston Grove.

The Ridgeway runs north-eastwards alongside a belt of trees. This marks the course of a disused railway – the Princes Risborough to Watlington line. Close to where the Ridgeway crosses the lane to Kingston Blount is the old level-crossing keeper's cottage. The National Trail route is also followed along this stretch by the Swans Way, the long-distance bridleway which links the Thames at Goring with Salcey Forest in Buckinghamshire. About a mile beyond the Kingston Blount lane is the old Chinnor cement works, below Crowell Hill.

The way back to Kingston Blount begins just before the cement works. Turn left down the track that leads north to join the B4009 road at Crowell. From the corner where stands the Shepherd's Crook pub and an attractive little flint church, turn left again along the main road back to the Cherry Tree.

 ### RIDGEWAY - CROWELL HILL TO WAIN HILL (2 MILES)

The Ridgeway path continues along the track past the cement works and then crosses the lane to Chinnor. A mile beyond there the National Trail leaves the old Icknield Way to curve east around the foot of Wain Hill.

BLEDLOW
The Lions of Bledlow
❧

*E*njoy splendid views throughout as we follow the National Trail along a winding footpath that climbs green pastures to Lodge Hill and then descends across open farmland. The outward route is along a clear trackway, the return route is by footpath. Other walks, both shorter and longer, can be planned from Bledlow, which is a good centre for exploring. The Ridgeway section included in this circular walk is from Wain Hill to Hemley Hill, a distance of 3 miles.

The villages of Bledlow and Bledlow Ridge, and the beechwood-covered hills between them, offer some of the prettiest scenery in south-east England. The Chinnor Hill Nature Reserve protects an abundance of valuable habitats and Bledlow Cross, on the slopes of Wain Hill, offers a curious turf-cut figure that has long interested archaeologists. In Bledlow village itself is a fine medieval church and an old paper mill set in a gorge-like valley where watercress beds once grew extensively.

The Lions of Bledlow occupies a 400 year old listed building and is a pub that should not be missed. It is recommended in many a pub guide and is well-known amongst walkers of the Chiltern Hills. It has a rambling interior, the one large bar room being split into separate sections by brick pillars and old oak posts and screens. Everywhere there are low beams, old settle seats, tiled floors, inglenooks and walls decorated with brasses, pictures, clocks and firearms. At the back is a restaurant, and a room with a dart board. Some say the building is haunted, and who knows? An old customer unwilling to leave perhaps.

This freehouse serves many real ales, including Ruddles, Theakston, Marston and Wadworth brews, Strongbow draught cider and a good selection of wines. The food on offer is wide ranging too and excellent quality. Regular items are supplemented by daily specials, chalked up on the blackboards, and children are given their own little choice. Vegetarians also will be well satisfied. Snacks include crusty bread rolls with different fillings, salads, soups and pâté; main meals range from chicken, plaice, steak and gammon to moussaka, quiche and pasta bake. Dessert options change daily but there are always mouthwatering ices, tarts, pastries and puddings. Normal pub opening times are kept, children are welcome and a pleasant beer garden provides a happy summertime venue. Telephone: 01844 343345.

- **HOW TO GET THERE:** Bledlow is 5 miles south-east of Thame and 10 miles north-west of High Wycombe. It stands just off the B4009, close to Princes Risborough. The Lions of Bledlow will be found west of the church.
- **PARKING:** There is a large pub car park. Vehicles can also be left along the roadside at the front and elsewhere in the village, provided no obstruction is caused.
- **LENGTH OF THE WALK:** 5½ miles. Map: OS Landranger 165 Aylesbury and Leighton Buzzard (inn GR: 777020).

THE WALK

The way to the Ridgeway path follows the gravel track that runs up beside the Lions of Bledlow, past the pub car park. However, those who wish, first, to visit Bledlow Cross, on the side of Wain Hill, and Chinnor Hill Nature Reserve should follow the footpath that cuts diagonally across the field. The Greek-style cross, cut into the chalk, measures 80 ft by 75 ft and can best be seen from the valley below. It is of unknown date, some experts saying it is prehistoric, others putting it no older than late 18th century. Some legends surround the figure; those climbing

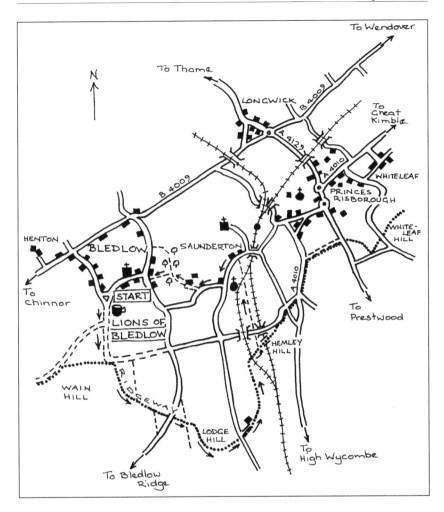

round it are supposedly given strength and virility. The nearby Nature Reserve, owned by the Berks, Bucks and Oxon Naturalists Trust, contains rare grassland habitats and plays host to many species of warblers. Public access is allowed but visitors are asked to be sensitive in their exploration of the site,which is of Special Scientific Interest.

The Ridgeway path is reached in about half a mile from the pub, the trackway there having climbed steadily under lines of trees. The signpost points left along the Icknield Way but the Ridgeway National Trail does not follow this route. Instead it goes through a kissing gate on the south side of the trackway and heads south-eastwards. As a narrow

71

grassy path it climbs at an angle over a grassy hillside. Up to the right are the wooded summits of the ridge, down to the left are views towards Aylesbury and across the Buckinghamshire Lowlands. The route is clearly marked by regular signposts and acorn disc symbols. Ignoring other footpaths either side follow the Ridgeway as it ascends gradually, goes through a kissing gate and continues along a field edge. Another kissing gate leads onto a country lane. Almost opposite, the Ridgeway continues across a field towards Lodge Hill, which by now is ahead. Several kissing gates are encountered on the way to the top. Lodge Hill is a pretty, wooded eminence run by English Nature. Butterfly habitats are preserved and the way has been carefully routed through the shrubland. From the summit wide views can be enjoyed in all directions. South are the rolling hills towards High Wycombe, north-eastwards the Chiltern ridge stretches over Whiteleaf Hill. In good weather the prospect is wonderful.

On the far side of Lodge Hill the Ridgeway descends, bears northward and is joined by a bridleway. Thereafter it follows the edge of a large field, goes under a line of pylons and meets a country lane. Crossing straight over this you follow it down the drive to a private house and then across the middle of a field beyond. After the next kissing gate it runs alongside a hedge, through a golf course, and then turns right to cross a railway line. Cross carefully, checking for passing trains. These directions may sound complicated but the way is clearly signposted throughout. Immediately ahead the land rises to Hemley Hill and the Ridgeway path continues straight on. But you leave the National Trail at this point and turn left.

The way back to Bledlow runs, initially, across the pasture to a stile and gate which will be found close to a large house. The track on the far side leads through the grounds to this house and out onto the road. You are, in fact, walking between two railway lines along this stretch. Cross over the road and continue northwards, at first by a broad hedgerow and later across the field. Running beside a deep wooded cutting the path eventually recrosses the railway line and follows a field edge all the way to Saunderton village. Turn left at the road. Beyond the Cherry Tree Nursing Home and lane to the church, which are both on the left, turn right down the road signposted to Bledlow. Where this road swings sharp left continue along the trackway straight on. This goes to a large farmstead. Where this track turns right at the barns go straight on, along a faint path that runs between two fields. At the distant hedge a stile will lead you through to a pathway that runs between the trees. This bears right and winds northwards through a woodland belt. Soon a clear path will be seen to the left, leading across the middle of a large field. Follow this to Bledlow village. At the road turn right and then, at the junction, left to reach the pub.

 RIDGEWAY - HEMLEY HILL TO WHITELEAF HILL (2½ MILES)

After crossing a second railway line, below Hemley Hill, the Ridgeway path joins a country lane that leads down to the A4010 road. From there it follows the main road to the outskirts of Princes Risborough and then turns right along a track. Keeping close to the houses it continues to the eastern suburbs from where it climbs Whiteleaf Hill.

ASKETT
The Black Horse
❧❧❧

A classic walk which includes a climb up to the broad summit of Whiteleaf Hill - a protected Nature Reserve. The going is steep but easy underfoot and worth it for the spectacular views. The Ridgeway section included in this circular walk is from Whiteleaf Hill to Pulpit Hill, a distance of 1½ miles. The outward route follows the lane through the pretty village of Whiteleaf; the return route follows a wide gravel trackway that descends from the wooded Pulpit Hill.

Askett is almost joined to Monks Risborough, where many thatched and timbered houses cluster around a handsome church that goes back to the 14th century. The lands hereabouts are said to have belonged to the monks of Christ Church, Canterbury, until Henry VIII's Reformation.

The Black Horse is not an old pub but it is a very traditional and friendly place. Inside there is one large bar room at the front, with brick fireplace surrounds and timberwork, and a small dining room at the back. The furniture is country-style and the walls are hung with ornaments. Outside there is a pleasant enclosed garden.

This is a Fuller's pub so real ales like ESB and London Pride are served. The draught cider is Scrumpy Jack and there are various wines on offer. The food here is especially inviting. The portions are large, the choice is wide and the prices are reasonable. Snacks include sandwiches, ploughman's lunches and smoked mackerel; main meals include grills, pies, various fish dishes and curries. The seafood platter is popular and vegetarian options range from chilli or pasta bake to spinach lasagne or nut and mushroom fettucini. Desserts are traditional with sweets like banana split, peach melba and spotted dick. The Black Horse keeps normal pub opening times. Telephone: 018444 345296.

• **HOW TO GET THERE:** Askett is 5 miles south of Aylesbury, standing on the A4010 road just outside Princes Risborough. The Black Horse is situated at the roundabout on the main road east of Askett village centre.

• **PARKING:** There is a pub car park. Vehicles can also be left along the lanes either side of the A4010, down to Askett and up to Lower Cadsden. The A4010 itself can be busy.

• **LENGTH OF THE WALK:** 4 miles. Map: OS Landranger 165 Aylesbury and Leighton Buzzard (inn GR: 819052).

THE WALK

From the Black Horse walk up the lane opposite and then, after about 500 yards and just before the Cadsden village sign, turn right along Upper Icknield Way. This takes you through the linear village of Whiteleaf. Do not hurry for there are many houses to admire. Beyond the large, detached early 20th century residences with their gables and Tudor features you pass the entrance to the Whiteleaf golf club and, in due course, the Red Lion pub. The southern end of the village contains the smaller, older cottages, many of which are thatched. All are different in character and age and cry out to be sketched, photographed or simply just admired at leisure. At the far end, at the T-junction, turn left up Peters Lane. Now begins the steep climb to the top of Whiteleaf Hill. Either keep to the lane, as it bends and curves its way to the summit, or else follow the second footpath on the left that you see after the right-hand bend. This narrow path climbs up a wooded slope at a steep angle. The summit of Whiteleaf Hill is an area managed as a nature reserve. The views are splendid with the lowlands of Oxfordshire and Buckinghamshire stretched out below. By following the Ridgeway along

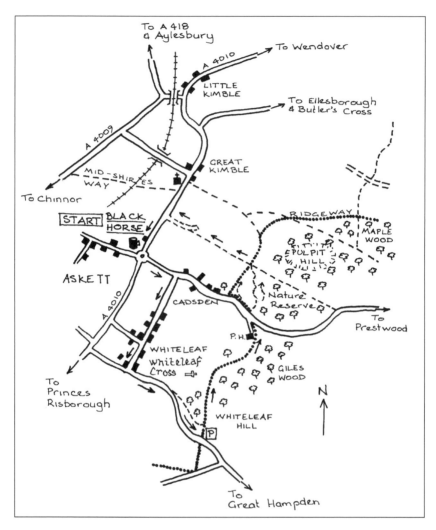

through the shrubbery, to a hill-top clearing, you reach an ancient burial mound. Close by, from the escarpment edge, you can look down upon the famous Whiteleaf Cross. This large chalk-cut figure looks down over Princes Risborough. It is some 80 ft long and across. Some say it is prehistoric with the original pyramid-shaped base being Iron Age and the cross-shaped top being added later in Saxon or even medieval times.

From close to the top of the cross, the Ridgeway path is signposted. A kissing-gate leads through to Giles Wood and the National Trail winds attractively down between the trees. At the bottom you emerge at a

The pretty village of Whiteleaf

lane, close to the Plough pub. Turn left. The Ridgeway proper actually continues 200 yards away on the right, climbing up through a copse and continuing across a field. However, a more pleasant alternative is signposted nearly opposite the Plough, through a staggered fence opening. This path winds through a wood and then crosses the Grangelands Nature Reserve. At the top edge of the Nature Reserve you meet a main track and various Ridgeway signposts. The footpath opposite climbs the base of Pulpit Hill through National Trust land, but you turn left here along the track marked as a bridleway.

The way back to Askett is very easy. Continue down the track. At the bottom, a rough tarmac track leads you down to the A4010. Turn left and walk the short way back to the Black Horse along a verge-way path.

 RIDGEWAY - PULPIT HILL TO MAPLE WOOD (½ MILE)

The Ridgeway path climbs the lower slopes of Pulpit Hill and skirts the bottom edge of the trees. Incidentally, it is from this part of the Ridgeway that paths link up with the Midshires Way long-distance route that connects the Chiltern Hills to the Pennines.

BUTLER'S CROSS

The Russell Arms

This pleasant walk circles the Chequers estate, offering glimpses of the house and parkland. The views throughout are wonderful, especially from the top of Coombe Hill. The Chilterns here are well-wooded and the route meanders between beech trees, oaks, ashes and sycamores adding variety to the landscape. A few steep gradients are encountered but the effort is well repaid. The Ridgeway section included in this walk is from Maple Wood to Coombe Hill, a distance of 2½ miles.

Butler's Cross is situated at the eastern end of Ellesborough village, a most pretty settlement with a collection of thatched cottages, 18th-century almshouses and a Norman-towered church. In this parish stands Chequers, the Prime Minister's country residence. Between Butler's Cross and Wendover is Wellwick Farm, dating from the 17th century and reputedly once the home of Judge Jeffreys, notorious for the 'Bloody Assizes'.

The Russell Arms is popular amongst locals and visitors alike for its traditional character, friendly atmosphere and wide selection of food and drink. Inside there is a large public bar with tiled floors, a cosy lounge at the back and, connected with that, a small dining room. These rooms are at different levels.

This is a Pubmaster establishment, serving real ales like Tetley Bitter, Flowers Original and ABC Best. Dry Blackthorn cider and a good selection of wines are also available. Snacks range from ploughman's lunches and salads to sandwiches and jacket potatoes; main meals include steak and kidney pie, gammon, fish dishes and pasta bakes. Daily specials are listed on a large blackboard in the lounge. Desserts include the traditional syrup sponge, spotted dick and a good selection of ices. The liqueur coffees are very much enjoyed. Normal opening times are kept, and a pleasant garden is used in summer. Telephone: 01296 622618.

- **HOW TO GET THERE:** Butler's Cross is 4 miles south of Aylesbury and less than 2 miles west of Wendover. It stands on the road that links Wendover to Ellesborough, which runs along the foot of the Chiltern escarpment. The Russell Arms will be found at the crossroads south of Terrick.
- **PARKING:** There is a car park outside the main entrance. Vehicles can also be left along the roadside nearby, provided no obstruction is caused.
- **LENGTH OF THE WALK:** 5 miles. Map: OS Landranger 165 Aylesbury and Leighton Buzzard (inn GR: 843071).

THE WALK

Outside the Russell Arms walk down the lane signposted to Great Kimble, travelling westwards, keeping the Chiltern escarpment over on the left-hand side. Very soon Ellesborough is reached, a pavement being provided all the way. Beyond the left bend keep to the tarmac path that climbs at an angle on the right. This leads to the church and those with time should look inside this fine building, which is largely 15th century.

The route continues on the south side of the road opposite the thatched cottage. Do not follow the track which is signposted as a footpath, but take the narrow path which crosses a field diagonally. It is reached through a kissing gate and is also signposted. This path climbs and skirts the western slopes of Beacon Hill. Down to the right amongst the trees, is Cymbeline's Castle (a Norman motte and bailey earthwork) and all around, the wider views begin to open out. Continue across the pastures, through a stile and then round and down to the bottom corner.

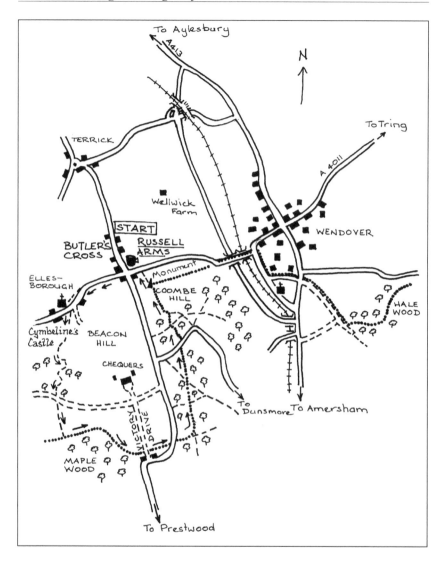

There another stile leads through to a clear pathway that winds round the top of a wooded combe. A long flight of steps then takes you up to a clearing which you cross along a rutted track. Follow this as it curves to another belt of woodland and proceeds under the trees, crossing over a wide earth track as it continues to a gate and stile. The countryside all around is beautiful. Ahead is Maple Wood, up to the right is the wooded Pulpit Hill, which is National Trust owned and topped by an Iron Age

The imposing monument atop Coombe Hill which commemorates the Boer War

hill fort. To the left the ground slopes down into the Chequers estate. From the gate and stile cross half-right diagonally over the field to reach the Ridgeway. Do not go through the kissing gate but turn left to follow the National Trail as signposted.

The Ridgeway runs down to the corner of Maple Wood and then bears right to follow the edge of a field, keeping the trees to the right. Down to the left is Chequers Court itself. This fine manor house, dating from the 15th century, was given to the nation after the Great War, to be used by the Prime Minister as a country retreat and conference centre. It was once the home of the Hawtrey family. The Ridgeway path is clearly marked as it skirts the Chequers estate, alongside Maple Wood and then down across Victory Drive that links the house with its lodge gates. The beech trees that line the drive were planted by Winston Churchill, to commemorate the end of the Second World War.

On the far side of Victory Drive the Ridgeway crosses the road to Great Missenden and climbs along a clear trackway up through a large woodland. Straight over a bridleway it continues as a footpath, still climbing fairly steeply. Towards the top it bears left and continues along the ridge, with a view through the trees to the left.

The next mile, all the way to Coombe Hill, is easy to follow. Despite many paths crossing through the woods, the Ridgeway is clearly marked with regular signposts, yellow arrows and acorn symbol discs. Across the country lane it continues, as a right then left dog-leg uphill. The last stretch, beyond a kissing gate, runs along a wide grassy path alongside the trees, with the views to the left. All around are gorse and dog rose bushes, oak and beech trees and – in good weather – many other people enjoying the views from this National Trust hilltop. At the far end is the monument that commemorates the Boer War. This is the highest viewpoint on the Chiltern part of the Ridgeway, and popular it deservedly has become. Over 800 feet high it commands a wide panorama, which is explained by a plaque close to the monument's base.

The way back to Butler's Cross is short but requires a little agility. Continue north from the monument, down a wide grassy path that descends steeply. Towards the bottom this path runs below a belt of ash trees to reach the road, where you turn left.

 ### RIDGEWAY - COOMBE HILL TO HALE WOOD (3½ MILES)

From Coombe Hill the Ridgeway path descends gradually to Wendover, where it runs through the streets of this pretty little town. Thereafter it climbs, by way of a wide track, to the western slopes of Cocks Hill. By footpath it then proceeds through woodlands, finally to contour into Hale Wood.

ST LEONARDS
The White Lion

Perfect for lovers of trees and leafy glades, this walk meanders through forest paths and returns along a quiet country lane. The Ridgeway section included is from Hale Wood to The Crong, a distance of 1½ miles. This stretch runs along the top (southern) edge of Wendover Woods, an area which the Forestry Commission has opened up to visitors.

The villages of St Leonards, Buckland Common, Cholesbury and Hawridge join together to produce a four-mile long settlement. This wends its way through the leafy uplands of the Chiltern escarpment behind Wendover Woods. There are many picturesque thatched cottages here and not a few handsome detached residences, and each village has its points of interest. Hawridge boasts an old windmill with sails (now a private house), Cholesbury has an Iron Age hill fort prettily circled by beech trees, and St Leonards has a charming little church.

The White Lion is a well-known local hostelry offering all the typical features of an English country pub – friendliness, good food and drink, and an old-fashioned atmosphere. The building is 17th century and has kept its old charm. Inside there is one main bar room but this is so arranged that different areas have separate identities. There is a dining area at one end, a 'snug' and small lounge at another, behind the chimney breast. There are beams, inglenooks and old wooden tables and chairs. Brasses, guns and farm implements decorate the walls, as well as original paintings, many of which are for sale.

This is a Benskins house selling Allied real ales together with other such guest beers as Greene King IPA and Red Rose. The draught cider is Addlestones and a good selection of wines is offered. Bar snacks served include sandwiches (plain and toasted) jacket potatoes and ploughman's lunches; main meals include steaks, various fish dishes, gammon, meat pies and cajun chicken. Vegetarians can choose such items as a broccoli bake or vegetable lasagne. Desserts range from apple pie and cherry cheesecake to old English puddings like spotted dick.

Normal pub opening times are kept; children are welcome and there is a pleasant garden to be used in summer months. Telephone: 01494 758387.

• **HOW TO GET THERE:** St Leonards is 3 miles east of Wendover and 3 miles south of Tring. It can also be reached quite easily from Chesham which is only 5 miles to the south-east. The White Lion stands on the border between St Leonards and Buckland Common.

• **PARKING:** There is a large pub car park. Vehicles can also be left in the few laybys nearby but parking spaces along the lanes in this area are not plentiful.

• **LENGTH OF THE WALK:** 5 miles. Map: OS Landranger 165 Aylesbury and Leighton Buzzard (inn GR: 918070).

THE WALK

Turn right outside the White Lion and walk north-westwards along the lane away from Buckland Common. For the first half mile there is, in fact, a choice of routes – both ending at St Leonard's attractive little church. The easy option is simply to keep to the road and walk through the village, admiring the selection of cottage architecture on the way. The slightly more adventurous option is to follow the footpaths that cut across the fields behind the village. Turning left at the stile and footpath signpost near the bungalow (beyond the Cholesbury Reservoir entrance) this latter route runs at an angle. It crosses the corner of a

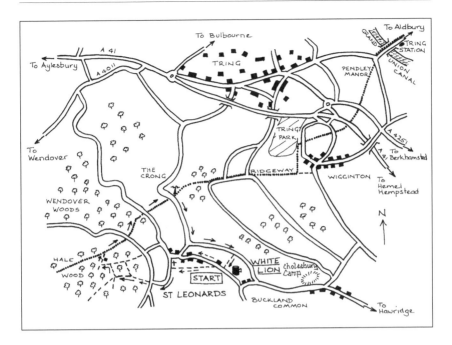

field, runs along by a line of trees and then cuts across the playing field behind the village hall. Thereafter it goes across two paddocks, to reach the road next to the church.

From St Leonard's church turn left down the road signposted to The Lee. This is a pretty, quiet lane. Be sure to admire Chapel Farm on the right, with its old courtyard and stables. After about half a mile you reach a T-junction. Cross straight over and continue on the far side along a gravel-and-grass trackway that curves to the woodland ahead. From this point pay careful attention since the route can be confusing. There are many forest paths here and one can lose one's sense of direction. Aiming for the north-western edge of the woodland keep left at the first fork and turn right at the junction of wide grassy trackways. In due course this brings you to a T-junction of tracks where you turn left. The path now narrows and winds between the trees. At the next main track turn right. This brings you to the forest edge. Up to now the trees have been largely coniferous. But the woodland you now approach, diagonally, across a field, is largely deciduous. It is Hale Wood and the Ridgeway lies ahead. As the path reaches Hale Wood it goes through a squeeze stile, round behind a large farmstead and down between the trees. At the Ridgeway turn right.

The wide earthy path here runs purposefully through the wood and you should take your time to savour the sights and sounds of the forest. At the road the Ridgeway continues almost opposite, uphill to the right slightly. You are now in the southern reaches of Wendover Woods where beech trees intermingle with oak to give a wonderfully dappled shade. Here and there a view opens up to the left, down the leafy combes. Further down the slopes the Forestry Commission has marked out various forest walks, bridleways and picnic areas and many people spend the day here wandering around enjoying the scenery. In actual fact, the highest point in the Chilterns (at 857 feet) is somewhere in these woods but the spot is not marked on the ground by any monument. The Ridgeway is well-signposted through this stretch. The path, at one point, turns left to descend into a steep valley (down some rough steps) and then turns right to follow a bridleway along the bottom of a gulley. This sunken track climbs steadily to the road. Across this the Ridgeway continues through a kissing gate next to a chalet bungalow. It is signposted. The route is now clear. You cross two fields and aim directly for the radio mast which marks the top of a hill known as The Crong. The wide views to the left are across the Vale of Aylesbury. When you meet the country lane turn right.

The way back to St Leonards is very straightforward. Continue down the lane for about a mile, keeping straight on at the road junction. Thereafter turn right along a signposted footpath. This crosses a single field to reach the road that you walked along at the start of the walk. Turn left for the White Lion.

RIDGEWAY - THE CRONG TO THE GRAND UNION CANAL (4 MILES)

The Ridgeway continues through Pavis Wood, to the village of Hastoe, where it joins a road. From there it follows a clear track to Wigginton and curves to run through woodlands at the edge of Tring Park. The A41 Tring bypass is crossed by footbridge. A woodside path takes the Ridgeway along by the grounds of Pendley Manor Hotel and down to the road near Tring Station. For most of this section the town of Tring can be seen. It is a pretty yet bustling town which should be explored.

BULBOURNE
The Grand Junction Arms

❧🕸❧

This walk covers various types of scenery from waterway to upland pasture, meadow to shrubland. The Ridgeway section included is from the Grand Union Canal to Pitstone Hill, a distance of 1½ miles. This pleasant stretch runs through the protected area of Duchies Piece and offers wide views towards Northamptonshire. The outward route uses a canal towpath, the return route follows a steep footpath down a wooded hillside.

Bulbourne is a little canalside hamlet with a row of cottages, a farm and a pub. Just north of the settlement is the well-known Tring Reservoirs National Nature Reserve and, along the road nearby, is the entrance to the College Lake Wildlife Reserve Centre. The whole area is a bird-watcher's paradise.

The Grand Junction Arms is a modernised Victorian-style pub popular amongst the narrow-boat fraternity. Inside there are many canal mementos: boating scene pictures decorate the walls and canalware pots, painted in 'Buckby' traditional patterns, stand by the fireplaces. There is one main bar room but the dining room is separate, being up some steps in an area that once formed part of the hayloft. The old stables are turned into a garden bar in summer, the gardens themselves being pleasantly located down by the canal.

This is a Greenalls house so Greenalls bitter is served as well as other real ales like Adnams, Bass and a weekly guest beer. Scrumpy Jack and Strongbow cider are offered and a full wine list, which includes a good 'draught' house wine. All the food is well cooked and wholesome. Snacks include homemade soups, 'lock-keeper's' lunch and 'bangers and mash'; main meals range from traditional pies and fish dishes to such interesting items as Irish whiskey pork and Scrumpy Jack chicken. Vegetarians can choose a pasta dish or something like mushroom, pepper and coconut curry. Normal pub opening times are kept and children are welcome. Telephone: 01442 890677.

• **HOW TO GET THERE:** Bulbourne stands just over a mile north of Tring town centre, on the B488 road to Ivinghoe and Dunstable. It is located on the Grand Union Canal, 6 miles from Berkhampsted. The Grand Junction Arms will be found on the north side of the B488.

• **PARKING:** There is a large pub car park. Few other parking places present themselves, the B488 being busy and devoid of lay-bys. Those undertaking the circular walk could park near Tring Station and pass the Grand Junction Arms during their excursion.

• **LENGTH OF THE WALK:** 4½ miles. Map: OS Landranger 165 Aylesbury and Leighton Buzzard (inn GR: 932136).

THE WALK

The walk along the tow-path begins opposite, across the road from the pub which, incidentally, is named after what this waterway was originally called – the Grand Junction Canal. It is a splendid stretch and time should be spared to watch the fish, birdlife and boating enthusiasts.

This part of the canal, between Marsworth and Berkhamsted, was completed in 1797. It cuts through the Chiltern escarpment as a summit level, with numerous locks either side taking the waterway down to the plain, the London Basin to the south and the Aylesbury Vale to the north. Just below Bulbourne two branch canals were constructed, the Wendover Arm (now largely gone) and the Aylesbury Arm. These also provide excellent walking opportunities for those wishing to explore the local countryside further.

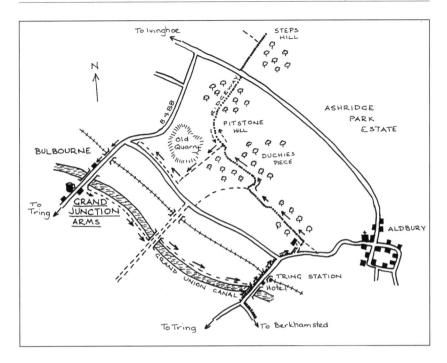

After little more than a mile, the tow-path reaches the road near Tring Station (having switched canal banks on the way). Here you join the Ridgeway National Trail, which is signposted.

Turn left along the road to walk past the Royal Hotel and Tring Station, crossing over the railway line. Ignoring Northfield Road on the left continue for 200 yards along the road towards Aldbury. The Ridgeway now leaves the tarmac to follow the concrete track that goes up to the left. Where this bends left continue up the grassy path to a Code of Respect board close to which the way goes through a gate and bears left. This is now an earthy bridleway that climbs at an angle through the woodland. The views begin to open out through the trees, left across Tring and straight on across Aylesbury.

In due course the Ridgeway leaves the bridleway and continues as a footpath, bearing right to climb to the edge of another woodland and then left to ascend a rough flight of steps. By this time you have entered Duchies Piece, an area protected by the Hertfordshire and Middlesex Wildlife Trust. The way is clearly marked by yellow arrows and guide posts as it wanders up and down between the beech and oak trees. At the edge of the woodland is a kissing gate, beyond which a path

The Grand Union Canal

descends to the left. This is the start of the route back to Bulbourne, but Pitstone Hill should be conquered first. This requires a short steep climb up grassland to the bumpy summit.

The way back follows the path that descends beside the woodland edge and wire fence. Beyond a stile continue down in the same direction across a pleasant area of shrubland, keeping the old quarry pit to the right. At the bottom you reach the road. Turn right, not along the road itself but along the path that runs parallel, beside the intervening hedgerow. At the far corner you join the B488 where you turn left for the Grand Junction Arms half a mile away.

 ### RIDGEWAY - PITSTONE HILL TO STEPS HILL (1 MILE)

The Ridgeway continues as a clear grassy path along the ridge, eventually to cross the lane linking Aldbury with Ivinghoe. The views to the left are superbly panoramic, the views to the right take in the Ashridge Park National Trust woodlands. Beyond the Aldbury lane the National Trail crosses open pastureland, below the ridge formed by the Ivinghoe Hills.

IVINGHOE
The Rose and Crown

An exhilarating walk to the top of Ivinghoe Beacon. Enjoy the wonderful views and look back at the escarpment that has carried the Ridgeway to this point. The final section included here, is from Steps Hill to Ivinghoe Beacon, a distance of 1½ miles. The outward route uses a clear footpath across farmland, with some steep gradients to be negotiated; the return route is, mostly, along a gravel trackway through pretty countryside.

Ivinghoe is an extremely pretty village with its fine 13th-century church (including some wonderful stone and wood carving), the 18th-century Old Brewery House (now a Youth Hostel) and a large collection of medieval and classical buildings. Across a field is Pitstone Windmill (National Trust), which was built in 1627 and is thought to be the oldest post mill in England. It is said that Sir Walter Scott took the name of this settlement as an inspiration for the name of his novel *Ivanhoe*.

The Rose and Crown, which is a freehouse, is justifiably well-known for its traditional atmosphere, friendliness and good selection of pub food. Inside there are two fairly small rooms, a lounge at the front and public bar with dartboard at the back. The decor is unpretentious: hunting prints decorate the walls and the rooms are furnished with wooden bench seats and metal tables. Outside there is a small paved area used in good weather.

Adnams and Morrells real ales are served and the draught cider is Gaynors Old English. A small selection of wines is also available. The food is all home cooked and the meat is bought at the local farm shop. Snacks include jacket potatoes and sandwiches (various fillings); main meals range from meat pies, casseroles, salads, curries and seafood platters to vegetable lasagnes and chilli. The desserts are wonderfully English, including apple and sultana pudding, spotted dick, treacle sponge and raspberry and redcurrant pie, these served with cream, custard or ice cream. Normal pub opening times are kept. Telephone: 01296 668472.

• **HOW TO GET THERE:** Ivinghoe is 6 miles south of Leighton Buzzard and 3 miles north of Tring, on the B489 road to Dunstable. The Rose and Crown stands in Vicarage Lane, in the northern part of the village.

• **PARKING:** There is no pub car park here but vehicles can be left along the neighbouring side-streets including Vicarage Lane itself where there are some official parking spaces.

• **LENGTH OF THE WALK:** 4½ miles. Map: OS Landranger 165 Aylesbury and Leighton Buzzard (inn GR: 945163).

THE WALK

Outside the Rose and Crown turn left up Vicarage Lane and then left again along the B489, to leave the village behind. There is a pavement along here. Ignoring the B488, that turns left to Dunstable, continue for about 50 yards beyond the road junction. Immediately before the second bungalow a footpath signpost points left. Follow the direction indicated, climbing the stile and proceeding alongside a hedge. Soon the open fields are reached and the hills ahead beckon.

The route to the Ridgeway is very clear. The footpath is fairly straight as it crosses the sheep pastures. It climbs steadily towards the wooded slope in front. Up to the left is Ivinghoe Beacon, behind and getting smaller is the Pitstone Windmill. In due course you follow the edge of a pretty little combe or dry valley, which is down to your immediate left.

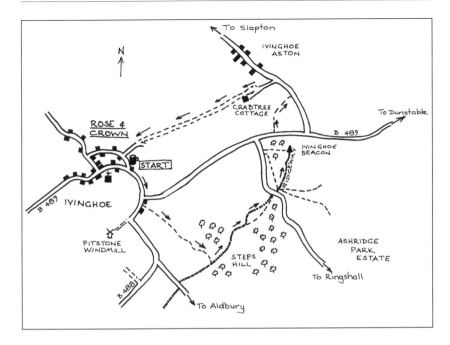

Half way up the slope you cross a stile and enter National Trust land. There is no obvious path but the Ridgeway is very close. Continue up until you join the National Trail as it comes in from the right.

The Ridgeway now proceeds to climb the ridge at an angle, towards the trees on the Steps Hill skyline. It skirts the top of the little combe, which is still down to the left, and ascends to a gate and stile. By this time the view is truly widening. Beyond Ivinghoe village you can see Mentmore Towers, the huge Victorian mansion which was once the home of the Rothschilds. To the right of that, further away, is Leighton Buzzard.

From the gate and stile there is a choice of routes. The Ridgeway proper curves to the left and proceeds along the top of the grassy slope, contouring round below the line of trees. The wide track beyond the stile and gate, on the other hand, continues through the woodlands of the Ashridge Estate. The former route avoids the stile and the latter route provides a pleasant stroll through shrublands and woods. The two routes meet again at the col, where the ridgetop dips and the road from Ringshall cuts through the Ivinghoe Hills.

Beyond this road the Ridgeway makes its last ascent, to the top of Ivinghoe Beacon. And there to greet your effort are a couple of stone

Ivinghoe Beacon

plinths, the remains of an Iron Age hill fort, the low mound of a prehistoric burial chamber and, best of all, a wonderful panorama.

The way back to Ivinghoe village begins down on the B489 below the Beacon. This can either be reached directly (down a very steep path that descends through thorny shrubland) or circuitously (back towards the Ringshall road and then a more gradual descent round the western slope of the hill). Close to the road junction a footpath signpost points north along the edge of a field. This is part of the Two Ridges Link, a footpath joining the Chilterns with the Greensand Ridge at Leighton Buzzard. Follow this to Ivinghoe Aston, the way running around the edge of the second field to meet the road close to a line of pylons. On that road turn left for the village in question. Here you leave the Two Ridges Link, for the easy walk back to the Rose and Crown. Just before the village name board turn left along a clear gravel trackway. This accompanies a private drive (to Crabtree Cottage), which is interestingly furnished with old lamp standards. The bridleway, for such it is, runs parallel to this drive and then, beyond the 'cottage', continues through pretty countryside part of which is now a golf course. Follow it all the way to Vicarage Lane and the Rose and Crown.

INFORMATION AND ACCOMMODATION

Various guides, leaflets and information packs are available from the following. These can also give general advice about facilities, transport and accommodation found along the Ridgeway.

National Trails Office, Countryside Service, Dept of Leisure and Arts, Holton, Oxford OX33 1QQ

Friends of the Ridgeway, 90 South Hill Park, London NW3 2SN

Icknield Way Association, 65 London Road, Hitchin, Hertfordshire SG4 7NE

Chiltern Society, 19 Valentine Way, Chalfont St Giles, Buckinghamshire HP8 4JB

Long Distance Walkers Association, 10 Temple Park Close, Leeds, West Yorkshire LS15 0JJ

Tourist Information can be obtained from the following Regional Tourist Boards. These can help with holiday planning and overnight accommodation booking.

West Country Tourist Board, 60 St Davids Hill, Exeter, Devon EX4 4SY. Tel: 01392 76351. (This covers Wiltshire. Tourist Information Centres also at Avebury, Marlborough and Swindon.)

Southern Tourist Board, 40 Chamberlayne Road, Eastleigh, Hampshire SO5 5JH. Tel: 01703 620006. (This covers Oxfordshire, Berkshire and Buckinghamshire. Tourist Information Centres also at Faringdon, Newbury, Wantage, Abingdon, Didcot, Wallingford, Reading, High Wycombe, Thame, Aylesbury, Princes Risborough and Wendover.)

East Anglian Tourist Board, Toppesfield Hall, Hadleigh, Suffolk IP7 5DN. Tel: 01473 822922. (This covers Hertfordshire. Tourist Information Centres also at Tring and Hemel Hempstead.)

There are four Youth Hostels along the Ridgeway. These provide simple, friendly accommodation at reasonable prices and can be booked directly. More general information about the YHA can be obtained from the South England Regional Office: 11B York Road, Salisbury, Wiltshire SP2 7AP. Telephone: 01722 337515.

YHA Ridgeway, The Court Hill Ridgeway Centre, Court Hill, Wantage, Oxfordshire OX12 9NE. Tel: 01235 760253

YHA Streatley-on-Thames, Hill House, Reading Road, Streatley, Reading, Berkshire RG8 9JJ. Tel: 01491 872278

YHA Bradenham, The Village Hall, Bradenham, High Wycombe, Buckinghamshire HP14 4HF. Tel: 01494 562929

YHA Ivinghoe, The Old Brewery House, Ivinghoe, Nr. Leighton Buzzard, Bedfordshire LU7 9EP. Tel: 01296 668251